CARDINAL
HUME
A Spiritual Companion

CARDINAL HUME

A Spiritual Companion

REFLECTIONS
THROUGH THE YEAR

Compiled by Liam Kelly

PARACLETE PRESS
BREWSTER, MASSACHUSETTS

Library of Congress Cataloging-in-Publication Data

Hume, Basil, 1923–1999
    Cardinal Hume : a spiritual companion.
      p. cm.
    ISBN 1-55725-268-8 (pbk.)
    1. Church year. 2. Catholic Church—Liturgy. 3. Spiritual life—Catholic Church. I. Title.
    BX1970 .H86 2001
    242'.3—dc21   00-011598

Scripture quotations are taken from the Revised Standard Version of the Bible, ©1946, 1952, 1971 by the Division of Christian Education of the National Council of the Churches of Christ in the USA. Used by permission.

"Lord of Surprises" reproduced from *Prayers for the Church Community*, compiled by Roy Chapman and Donald Hilton, with the permission of the National Christian Education Council.

Excerpts from the English translation of *The Roman Missal* ©1973, International Committee on English in the Liturgy, Inc. All rights reserved.

"Mary, Mother of Jesus" by Dante Alighieri, tr. R.A. Knox, used by permission of Burns & Oates.

Prayers from *Love on the Cross* by Richard Garrard © Kevin Mayhew Ltd. Used by permission. License No. 009050

"Christmas" by John Betjeman, from *Collected Poems*, used by permission of John Murray (Publishers) Ltd.

Original edition published in England under the title *Cardinal Hume: A Spiritual Companion* by Lion Publishing plc, Oxford, England.
© Lion publishing plc 2000
Text copyright ©2000 The Literary Estate of Cardinal Basil Hume

The author asserts the moral right to be identified as the author of this work. Compiled by Liam Kelly

This edition published by Paraclete Press, 2001
ISBN 1-55725-268-8

10 9 8 7 6 5 4 3 2 1

Brewster, Massachusetts
www.paracletepress.com

Printed in the United States of America.

Contents

Introduction

For many people I believe 17 June 1999 will become, if it has not already, one of those "Where were you when…?" dates. In the late afternoon of that day, Cardinal George Basil Hume died peacefully. The next day's newspapers would have embarrassed him: "Cardinal who was a spiritual inspiration to people of all faiths dies of cancer aged 76" "Cardinal Hume, a spiritual healer of history's divisions," "Cardinal Hume, 'a true holy man,' dies," and, "He was a gentle, wise man who loved football and fishing. He was also an outstanding spiritual leader.… and the way he faced death was a testament to the strength of his faith."

I suspect that for many of those closest to Cardinal Hume—and perhaps, too, many not so close—some part of the world ended on 17 June. I had the privilege of getting to know the Cardinal as a friend over a period of some years, and for my part I know that his death was—is—very hard to take. Despite what many might perceive as his exalted position as leader of the Catholic Church in England and Wales, what characterized Cardinal Hume was a simplicity and humility that shone through in all that he did and said. As has been written time and time again, he had the ability to befriend people, to let them know that they were important, and that he could devote time to them. Often he used to say to me, "Never forget, we are dealing with people first of all, not principles." In an article in *The Times* shortly after Cardinal Hume's death, Dr. Jonathan Sacks, the Chief Rabbi, wrote: "When I think of Cardinal Hume, I recall the words of Judaism's early sages. They asked: 'Who is a hero?' They answered: 'One who turns strangers into friends.' That was his great gift. He drew people to him by his love of God and his deep feeling for humanity. While you were with him, you felt enlarged. He was a friend, and we were lucky to have him. . . . Serene in life, serene in the face of death, Cardinal Hume was a man of God who turned strangers into friends."

Cardinal Hume. A man of God. When the Cardinal announced that he had cancer, he had said, "Above all, no fuss." How he must have smiled at the endless fuss since then! But, more importantly, he also said: "I have received two wonderful graces. First, I have been given time to prepare for a new future. Second, I find myself—uncharacteristically—calm and at peace." Preparing for a new future was, in many respects, the whole theme of Cardinal Hume's life. It is the theme of everybody's life. He often spoke of our life here on earth as a pilgrimage, a journey towards God. He once wrote: "The pilgrim through life's journey needs light for guidance along the road that leads to our true and final home. That pilgrim is you, and that pilgrim is me, often confused and often wounded" (*To Be a Pilgrim*).

To me, and many others, Cardinal Hume was and still is our pilgrim friend—our companion on the journey, searching along with us. Our thanks are to God for gifting us such a travelling companion.

Liam Kelly
October 1999

How to Use This Book

A Spiritual Companion is, quite simply, what the title suggests. It is an invitation to journey towards God, to make our own personal pilgrimage to our Creator. The book follows the seasons of the Christian year. There is a brief introduction to each season, followed by reflective material for the different weeks and sometimes different days of the season in question—first a reflection by Cardinal Hume, followed by prayers and poems from other sources and by scripture passages: all elements which can be used to accompany us on our spiritual journey. Read them, reflect on them, return to them, so that they can nourish the search for God.

The great feast for the Christian churches is that of Easter, celebrating the resurrection of Jesus from the dead. *A Spiritual Companion* begins, then, with preparation for that feast through Ash Wednesday and the season of Lent. The Easter theme is continued and culminates in the feast that is often called the "birthday of the church," Pentecost. More prayers, reflections and scripture passages are offered on a number of themes—called here "The Season of Quiet Reflection"—before we arrive at the season of Advent. This is preparation for Christmas, when we celebrate the birth of Jesus. And *A Spiritual Companion* concludes with two more great feasts that close the Christmas season: the Epiphany and the Baptism of the Lord. This spiritual journey is one undertaken in search of the God who is our friend. May *A Spiritual Companion* nourish you and sustain you on your path.

Acknowledgments

I would like to thank Charles Wookey, Cardinal Hume's Public Affairs assistant, for his help in facilitating the compilation of this book. I would also like to acknowledge Heather Craufurd, who typed up the Cardinal's talks with such devotion over many years and whose work has made my task so much easier.

Liam Kelly

Holiness involves friendship with God.
The movement towards the realization of God's love for us
is similar to our relationship with other people.
There comes a moment, which we can never quite locate
    or catch,
when an acquaintance becomes a friend.
In a sense, the change from one to the other
has been taking place over a period of time.
But there comes a point when
we know we can trust the other, exchange confidences,
keep each other's secrets: We are friends.
There has to be a moment like that in our relationship
    with God.
He ceases to be just a Sunday acquaintance
and becomes a weekday friend.

Cardinal Hume, The Mystery of Love

The Season of Lent

❦

Sometimes people ask each other, "Did you have a good Lent?" Of course, it is unclear what a "good" Lent precisely entails, and it might seem somewhat strange to be using the word "good" about a season traditionally associated with penance, fasting, and self-denial. On its own, Lent is meaningless. It is a time of preparation for the great feast of Easter, the most important feast in the Christian calendar, celebrating the death and resurrection of Jesus Christ.

The word "lent" comes from the Anglo-Saxon word for springtime, *lencten*. March was the *lencten monath*, a clear association with the lengthening of days and the transition from winter to spring. For the early Christians, preparation for Easter involved a two-day period of fasting. The latter meant complete abstention from food for the whole or part of the designated fasting period. The fast in preparation for Easter was gradually extended to the whole of Holy Week, and by the fourth century was observed in many places as a forty-day period, reflecting Jesus' forty-day fast in the desert recorded in St. Matthew's Gospel.

Fasting as a penitential practice is aimed at strengthening the spiritual life through self-denial. However, it is only one aspect of the season of Lent. As preparation for Easter, this period offers an opportunity to reflect on the meaning of Jesus' own suffering, death, and resurrection. This is reflected in the popular traditional religious devotion known as the "Way" or "Stations of the Cross," a practice recalling events on Jesus' journey to Calvary. Easter is also the time when new Christians are often welcomed into the church, and so Lent is a special time of preparation for them, and a time for Christians already baptized to reflect on the meaning of their own baptism, ready then to renew their baptismal vows. Finally, Lent is also a time for repentance and conversion. This is reflected in the somber color purple which is used for church vestments during Lent. There is also great emphasis on seeking forgiveness for sins, especially in the sacrament of confession or reconciliation.

Ash Wednesday

Lent begins on Ash Wednesday. The day before is known as "Shrove Tuesday" or "Mardi Gras," two important titles. The former comes from the Middle English word *shriven*, "confession," and refers to the practice of going to confession in preparation for Lent. "Mardi Gras," a French phrase literally meaning "Fat Tuesday," stems from the practice of celebrating the last day before the rigors of Lent set in. It was a day of carnival, from the Latin *carnevalarium*, "removal of meat," when many of the foods that could not be eaten during the Lenten fast were used up.

The name "Ash Wednesday" refers to the practice of placing ashes on the forehead on this day as a sign of repentance. The sign of the cross is made with the ashes and one of two prayers is said: "Remember, you are dust and unto dust you will return," or, "Turn away from sin and be faithful to the gospel." In this spirit the season of Lent begins.

Today we begin Lent; it is Ash Wednesday. . . . I will admit to you that the Ash Wednesday ceremony, the blessing and distribution of the ashes, is, of all the ceremonies in the year, the one that I do with the least enthusiasm. It is rather a chilling ceremony, but it shows the realism of the church and reminds us very bluntly and very starkly that we are ashes and unto ashes we shall return. It is a chilling thought but a very salutary one. So although I recognize that it is not by any manner of means my favorite ceremony, I recognize just how important that reminder is. So during Lent there is always a process of turning more to God and therefore away from those things that separate us from God, or interrupt our service of him, indeed our love of him.

A turning to God. Therefore how important it is in planning our Lent that there should be resolutions of a very positive nature. . . . It was St. Paul who said: "God loves a cheerful giver," and cheerfulness is a characteristic of a real Christian. So let our Lent be not only cheerful, but deeply joyous, because we have determined to turn to God, and we know that to turn to God is to receive an outpouring of his love, and when we receive an outpouring of his love, then we are at peace and can be useful instruments in his service.

Cardinal Hume, Ash Wednesday, Westminster Cathedral, 1977

Prayer

Father in heaven,
the light of your truth bestows sight
to the darkness of sinful eyes.
May this season of repentance
bring us the blessing of your forgiveness
and the gift of your light.

Alternative Opening Prayer, Ash Wednesday, Roman Missal

Is this a Fast, to keep
    The larder lean?
      And clean
From fat of veals and sheep?

Is it to quit the dish
    Of flesh, yet still
      To fill
The platter high with fish?

Is it to fast an hour,
    Or ragg'd to go,
      Or show
A down-cast look and sour?

No: 'tis a Fast to dole
    Thy sheaf of wheat
      And meat
Unto the hungry soul.

It is to fast from strife
    And old debate,
      And hate;
To circumcise thy life.

To show a heart grief-rent;
    To starve thy sin,
      Not bin;
And that's to keep thy Lent.

Robert Herrick (1591-1674),
"To Keep a True Lent"

Scripture

"Yet even now," says the Lord,
"return to me with all your heart,
with fasting, with weeping, and with mourning;
and rend your hearts and not your garments."
Return to the Lord, your God,
for he is gracious and merciful,
slow to anger, and abounding in steadfast love,
and repents of evil.

*This was written by the prophet Joel, possibly about 400 BC,
encouraging the people to stop being unfaithful to God. The prophet
declared that if they turned to penance and prayer then the kingdom
of Judah might flourish again: Joel 2:12-13*

Blessed is the man
who walks not in the counsel of the wicked,
nor stands in the way of sinners,
nor sits in the seat of scoffers;
but his delight is in the law of the Lord,
and on his law he meditates day and night.

Psalm 1:1-2

First Week of Lent

Perhaps one particular question we can ask ourselves: Is our religion something only external, or does it touch our minds and our hearts? What is important about Lent is to have a change of heart; put things right in our lives which may be wrong. I sum that up by saying: to turn ourselves away from those things that separate us from God or displease him, and allow him to touch our minds and hearts. Because when the great feast of Easter comes—and Lent is the preparation for Easter—we need to be fully prepared to receive the graces which God will want to give us at that time.

Cardinal Hume, Ash Wednesday, Westminster Cathedral, 1996

Prayer

Father, we begin our Lenten journey to you.
As we set out on the path that your Son took
to his death and resurrection,
may we reflect his journey in our own lives.

His fast of forty days
makes this a holy season of self-denial.
By rejecting the devil's temptations
he has taught us
to rid ourselves of the hidden corruption of evil,
and so to share his paschal meal in purity of heart,
until we come to its fulfilment
in the promised land of heaven.

Preface of First Sunday of Lent, Roman Missal

Each year you give us this joyful season
when we prepare to celebrate the paschal mystery
with mind and heart renewed.
You give us a spirit of loving reverence for you, our Father,
and of willing service to our neighbor.
As we recall the great events that gave us new life in Christ,
you bring the image of your Son to perfection within us.

Preface of Lent I, Roman Missal

Scripture

Have mercy on me, O God,
according to thy steadfast love;
according to thy abundant mercy
   blot out my transgressions.
Wash me thoroughly from my iniquity,
and cleanse me from my sin!

Create in me a clean heart, O God,
and put a new and right spirit within me.
Cast me not away from thy presence,
and take not thy Holy Spirit from me.
Restore to me the joy of thy salvation,
and uphold me with a willing spirit.

O Lord, open thou my lips,
and my mouth shall show forth thy praise.

Psalm 51:1-2, 10-12, 15

Second Week of Lent

We must allow ourselves to be inspired. For my part, this year it will be the text from St. John's Gospel: "As the Father has loved me, so I have loved you. Abide in my love." Let those words of our Lord ring in our ears and sing, so to speak, in our hearts. Surely you want to get to know the person who said that? Surely we want to reflect on that and pray about it, to inspire us in our lives and give us peace and comfort? All the more so when we come to reflect on our Lord's message to each one of us: "Repent and believe the gospel."

Cardinal Hume, Ash Wednesday, Westminster Cathedral, 1999

Prayer

God our creator,
you always listen to those who call to you.
Hear our prayer,
and may your help prevent us from becoming absorbed
in material things.

Merciful God
we thank you for your merciful love for us;
may we whom you have forgiven learn to forgive
and be reconciled with those we fear, despise, and hate.

Adapted from Richard Garrard, Love on the Cross

Scripture

Brethren, join in imitating me, and mark those who so
live as you have an example in us. For many, of whom I
have often told you and now tell you even with tears, live
as enemies of the cross of Christ. Their end is destruction,
their god is the belly, and they glory in their shame, with
minds set on earthly things. But our commonwealth is in
heaven, and from it we await a Saviour, the Lord Jesus
Christ, who will change our lowly body to be like his
glorious body.

*St. Paul may have written this letter to the people of Philippi while
imprisoned in Rome in AD 61-63. In the letter he encourages the
people to be thankful for the good news they have received and
model themselves on Jesus Christ: Philippians 3:17-21a*

Third Week of Lent

It is important to reflect on how we face up to the cross in our lives. In a way, we train for it during Lent by imposing some self-denial, some sacrifice, on ourselves—what we call "giving up something for Lent." That may sound negative and in many ways it is. But we must remember that it is done in order to help us turn to God in prayer, to focus our minds on him, and raise our hearts in desire for him. Whatever happens to us is allowed by him in order that we should draw closer to him, for that is the one thing Almighty God wants: that we should be close to him and that he should be close to us.

Cardinal Hume, The Mystery of the Cross

Prayer

Father,
you have taught us to overcome our sins
by prayer, fasting, and works of mercy.
When we are discouraged by our weakness,
give us confidence in your love.

Opening Prayer, Third Sunday of Lent, Roman Missal

Scripture

Make me to know thy ways, O Lord;
teach me thy paths.
Lead me in thy truth, and teach me,
for thou art the God of my salvation;
for thee I wait all the day long.
Be mindful of thy mercy, O Lord,
and of thy steadfast love,
for they have been from of old.
Remember not the sins of my youth,
    or my transgressions;
according to thy steadfast love
    remember me,
for thy goodness' sake, O Lord!
Good and upright is the Lord;
therefore he instructs sinners in the way.
He leads the humble in what is right,
and teaches the humble his way.

Psalm 25:4-9

Fourth Week of Lent

One of the purposes of Lent is to make adjustments, to
question our attitude towards sin. Am I compromising?
Am I being too easy in breaking God's law? Is my way of
life too exclusively worldly? What are my values; what is
really important? . . . We look forward already to the
celebration of Easter and the resurrection of Jesus Christ.
There comes a point in that ceremony when we shall
note we have come to the end of our Lenten observances,
and it is good at that moment to be able to look back and
say: Yes, I did do my best this Lent in preparation for this
great feast of Easter.

Cardinal Hume, Ash Wednesday, Westminster Cathedral, 1991

Prayer

Father of peace,
we are joyful in your Word,
your Son Jesus Christ,
who reconciles us to you.
Let us hasten towards Easter
with the eagerness of faith and love.

Opening Prayer, Fourth Sunday of Lent, Roman Missal

Grant us, O Lord, the grace to remain alert in your service, to be ready to meet you in people and events of this life, and to meet you at last in heaven.

Richard Garrard, Love on the Cross

Scripture

Thus says the Lord: "In a time of favor I have answered you; in a day of salvation I have helped you . . . saying to the prisoners, 'Come forth,' to those who are in darkness, 'Appear.' They shall feed along the ways, on all bare heights shall be their pasture. . . . But Zion said, 'The Lord has forsaken me; my Lord has forgotten me.' Can a woman forget her sucking child, that she should have no compassion on the son of her womb? Even these may forget, yet I will not forget you."

This part of the book of Isaiah was written maybe 500 years before the time of Jesus. The Jewish people were in exile in Babylon and the prophet tried to console them and hoped that they would trust in God: Isaiah 49:8a, 9, 14-15

So Jesus proclaimed, as he taught in the temple, "You know me, and you know where I come from? But I have not come of my own accord; he who sent me is true, and him you do not know. I know him, for I come from him, and he sent me." So they sought to arrest him; but no one laid hands on him, because his hour had not yet come.

From St. John's Gospel, written towards the end of the first century: John 7:28-30

Fifth Week of Lent

During this Lent period we should be reflecting on our
Lord's suffering and death and in our prayer ask him
through the Holy Spirit to help us try to have a little
understanding and a greater appreciation of what it was
he did for us. But it remains one of God's secrets of which
we can only have a little glimpse. In that gospel passage
our Lord went on to say: "If any man will come after me,
let him deny himself, take up his cross daily and follow
me." Again, it is right in Lent that we should reflect on
the role of the cross in our lives. There is no human life
that is ever totally free of some suffering or pain. It may
be something quite trivial, a little anxiety, worry; on the
other hand something much greater and long lasting
which could be a great burden. It is good to remember
when we have to endure pain that our Lord said: "If you
want to be my disciple, deny yourself; take up your cross
daily and follow me. . . ." I remember being told two
things about the cross in our lives; both have been very
helpful. First: The real cross is the one you have not
chosen, the one that doesn't fit neatly on your shoulder.
That is a very authentic cross and so very difficult to
accept. The other: A Mother Superior said to one of her
community who was grumbling about the cross she had
to carry: "Don't drag your cross, carry it." There is a lot of
wisdom in that.

Cardinal Hume, Parish Visitation, Carmelite Church, March 5, 1992

Prayer

God of grace and mercy
we rejoice in your love and give thanks
that you accept the poor devotion of our lives.

Richard Garrard, Love on the Cross

Father,
help us to be like Christ your Son,
who loved the world and died for our salvation.
Inspire us by his love,
guide us by his example,
who lives and reigns with you and the Holy Spirit,
one God, for ever and ever.

Opening Prayer, Fifth Sunday of Lent, Roman Missal

Scripture

But one of them, Caiaphas, who was high priest that year, said to them, "You know nothing at all; you do not understand that it is expedient for you that one man should die for the people, and that the whole nation should not perish." He did not say this of his own accord, but being high priest that year, he prophesied that Jesus should die for the nation, and not for the nation only, but to gather into one the children of God who are scattered abroad. So from that day on they took counsel how to put him to death.

Jesus therefore no longer went about openly among the Jews, but went from there to the country near the wilderness, to a town called Ephraim; and there he stayed with the disciples.

Now the Passover of the Jews was at hand, and many went up from the country to Jerusalem before the Passover, to purify themselves. They were looking for Jesus and saying to one another as they stood in the temple, "What do you think? That he will not come to the feast?"

John 11:49-56

Holy Week

⚮

The week preceding Easter has a number of names: Today it is popularly called "Holy Week," the Eastern Catholic Church calls it the "Week of Salvation," and early Christians spoke of the "Great Week." The framework for the week developed in Jerusalem where the actual sites of the historical passion, death, and resurrection of Jesus are located. A pilgrimage diary, written c. AD 381-84 by a lady called Egeria, describes many of the religious services of the week in Jerusalem. These rites were then brought to Europe in subsequent centuries.

Originally, the whole celebration was about one day: The Easter Vigil, starting at sunset on the eve of the sabbath and continuing until dawn on the first day of the week, Sunday, was *the* celebration of the resurrection of Jesus. Gradually, the celebration was extended to three days, beginning on the Friday, the day of the Lord's death. Later on, Thursday, too, was included, thus marking the day of the Lord's Supper. This period from Thursday evening is known as the "Sacred Triduum" (from the Latin for "three days.")

Holy Week begins with Palm Sunday. The day recalls Jesus' entry into Jerusalem, when the people "spread their garments on the road, and others cut branches from the trees and spread them on the road" (Matthew 21:8). In many churches today, palm branches are blessed, and the Gospel account of Jesus' triumphant entry into Jerusalem is proclaimed. But then the story of Jesus' Passion is also read, a reminder that this is the start of the week recalling these events, the start of Jesus' passage from death to new life.

Holy Week continues with the days of preparation of Monday, Tuesday, and Wednesday. In the past these were often days when people went to confession before the start of the Triduum on Holy Thursday evening. Wednesday was traditionally called "Spy Wednesday," the day on which Judas agreed to betray Jesus.

The proper name for Holy Thursday is Thursday of the Lord's Supper. It recalls the events in the Gospel concerning the Last Supper, when Jesus offered his body and blood to those at table, and also his washing of the disciples' feet at that meal. The love he showed, he told them, was a "new commandment." The Latin word mandatum, "commandment," has led to this day's also being called Maundy Thursday. In churches today there are special evening celebrations recalling Jesus' institution of the Eucharist, the Mass.

The following day, Good Friday, is the day on which Jesus died on the cross. The origins of the name "Good" are unknown, but it could be a reminder, on this day of mourning, that Jesus' death was in fact a saving event. Church services take place in the afternoon or early evening, with the focus again on the reading of the Passion from the Gospel and the veneration of the cross: "This is the wood of the cross on which hung the Saviour of the world."

Palm Sunday

Today, Palm Sunday, we remember how the crowds went out to meet Christ calling out: "Blessed is he who comes in the name of the Lord." Then we listen to that part of the gospel which describes the Passion and death of our Lord. This week, then, we are to set out to meet Christ in his passion, in those last days of his suffering.

We go out to meet him first, in order to follow him. He said to us: "If you want to be my disciple, you must deny yourself, take up your cross, and follow me." So in what we read in the gospel story and from our own experience of life and what is going on in the world around us, the experience of the world's suffering is taken by Christ in order to sanctify it, to give it meaning and significance. This week, almost hour by hour, we can follow Christ in those moments of his Passion.

It is good, then, to decide now that this is indeed going to be a Holy Week, a different week, a week when we meet Christ in his Passion, in order that when the resurrection is celebrated we can, after Easter Sunday, follow him more closely and witness to him—Christ who suffered, died, and rose from the dead.

Cardinal Hume, Palm Sunday, Westminster Cathedral, 1997

Prayer

Lord,
increase the faith of your people
and listen to our prayers.
Today we honor Christ our triumphant King
by carrying these branches.
May we honor you every day
by living always in him,
for he is Lord for ever and ever.

Alternative Prayer at the Blessing of Palms,
Roman Missal

Scripture

Lift up your heads, O gates!
and be lifted up, O ancient doors!
that the King of glory may come in.
Who is this King of glory?
The Lord of hosts,
he is the King of glory!

Psalm 24:9-10

Christ Jesus, who, though he was in the form of God, did
not count equality with God a thing to be grasped, but
emptied himself, taking the form of a servant, being born
in the likeness of men. And being found in human form
he humbled himself and became obedient unto death,
even death on a cross. Therefore God has highly exalted
him and bestowed on him the name which is above every
name, that at the name of Jesus every knee should bow, in
heaven and on earth and under the earth, and every
tongue confess that Jesus Christ is Lord, to the glory of
God the Father.

Philippians 2:5b-11

Monday in Holy Week

Tragedy and triumph are opposites. We think of them as strangers to each other. Yet, if we look more closely with the eyes of faith perhaps we can see just that they are not so much strangers as possibly even companions. Because the tragedy of Christ's death led to his triumphant resurrection.

It can be so in human experience, for life's tragedies, agonies, anguishes, and sorrows contain within themselves the possibility of new life and new hope.

So during the course of this Holy Week our task is not only to remember Christ's passion and death but to recognize the result of that for our lives, for through that death and resurrection have been given to us new life and new hope. So all the burdens of our lives will lead to little personal triumphs where we share more closely in Christ's life and enjoy the hope of future life which he has given to us.

Cardinal Hume, Palm Sunday, 1992

Prayer

The suffering and death of your Son
brought life to the whole world,
moving our hearts to praise your glory.
The power of the cross reveals your judgment on
    this world
and the kingship of Christ crucified.
The days of his life-giving death and glorious
    resurrection are approaching.
This is the hour when he triumphed over Satan's pride,
the time when we celebrate the great event of our redemption.

Adaptation of Preface of The Passion of the Lord, I and II,
Roman Missal

Scripture

Behold my servant, whom I uphold, my chosen, in whom
my soul delights; I have put my Spirit upon him; he will
bring forth justice to the nations. He will not cry or lift
up his voice, or make it heard in the street; a bruised reed
he will not break, and a dimly burning wick he will not
quench; he will faithfully bring forth justice. He will not
fail or be discouraged till he has established justice in the
earth; and the coastlands wait for his law.

This section of the book of Isaiah is sometimes referred to as the
"Book of Consolation": Isaiah 42:1-4

Tuesday in Holy Week

Only Christ could give the kind of love which can satisfy
God the Father's own longing to be loved. That is a
remarkable and deep thought. Only Jesus Christ can give
to the Father the love which the Father wants to receive.
And the other great secret revealed to us, and yet can
never be fully understood by us, is that God the Father
wanted to restore to us the privilege, the dignity, the joy
of being his beloved sons and daughters. And why? So
that we can share in Christ's love for the Father. So Jesus
Christ, the second Person of the Blessed Trinity, became
man and shared our life, shared our problems, in order
that we should be able as sons and daughters of God, to
give back love where love has first been given.

Cardinal Hume, Palm Sunday, 1979

Prayer

Father,
as we draw to the end of our Lenten journey,
may our eyes be fixed ever more firmly
on your Son, Jesus Christ,
who died on the cross to save us all.

Scripture

And he said to me, "You are my servant, Israel, in whom I will be glorified." But I said, "I have labored in vain; I have spent my strength for nothing and vanity; yet surely my right is with the Lord, and my recompense with my God."

And now the Lord says, who formed me from the womb to be his servant, to bring Jacob back to him, and that Israel might be gathered to him, for I am honored in the eyes of the Lord, and my God has become my strength—he says: "It is too light a thing that you should be my servant to raise up the tribes of Jacob and to restore the preserved of Israel; I will give you as a light to the nations, that my salvation may reach to the end of the earth."

The prophet Isaiah, the "Book of Consolation": Isaiah 49:3-6

Wednesday in Holy Week

There are, in today's world, innumerable signs of the denial of God. We do not need to look far for them. Nonetheless that same world, according to Paul VI, does in fact search for him "in unexpected ways." Among them we may count the pursuit of power, of riches, of uncontrolled pleasure— each of these can so dominate our minds and hearts, that we turn them, unthinkingly and uncritically, into false gods. We make them ends to be pursued for their own sakes, not means to achieve other and better goods. And they can so easily destroy those who have dedicated their lives to them. But the instinct to pursue that which we see to be best for ourselves is deep and strong. It is an instinct that may move us, when we heed its nobler prompting, to look for a treasure which is proof against corruption. That instinct is the effect of the need for something which is greater and nobler than ourselves. The treasure is God himself.

Cardinal Hume, Light in the Lord—Reflections on Priesthood

Prayer

"Forgive me Lord," he could have prayed
on this most black of days,
"For thirty silver pieces, Lord,
I sold your life away."

And Jesus, even on his cross,
could set him free from sin,
but Judas feared forgiveness more
than guilt and hate within.

To find our God a soul requires,
not perfectness of life,
but openness that owns the need
for healing from sin's blight.

Because he wished to master Christ
and chose the way of pride
he sealed himself away from love,
condemned himself and died.

Richard Garrard, Love on the Cross

Scripture

Then one of the twelve, who was called Judas Iscariot, went to the chief priests and said, "What will you give me if I deliver him to you?" And they paid him thirty pieces of silver. And from that moment he sought an opportunity to betray him. . . .

When it was evening, he sat at table with the twelve disciples; and as they were eating, he said, "Truly, I say to you, one of you will betray me." And they were very sorrowful, and began to say to him one after another, "Is it I, Lord?" He answered, "He who has dipped his hand in the dish with me, will betray me. The Son of man goes as it is written of him, but woe to that man by whom the Son of man is betrayed! It would have been better for that man if he had not been born." Judas, who betrayed him, said, "Is it I, Master?" He said to him, "You have said so."

The author of this gospel was writing probably five or ten years after the destruction of the Temple in Jerusalem, which happened in ad 70:
Matthew 26:14-16, 20-25

Holy Thursday

There seems to be no limit to the courtesies which Jesus wants to show us, his followers. What other motive could he have had, other than courtesy and love, in washing the feet of his apostles? That sign of love and courtesy they could readily see and understand, so it made easier the understanding of that other sign of love, the giving of his body to eat and his blood to drink. It was his love for us which inspired both actions—the washing of feet and the giving of Holy Communion.

This evening we commemorate both events. The external gestures and the words have much to say to us, but it is to their inner meaning that we must go. That understanding does not come all at once. It is a process, gradual, and for the most part, slow. So go to him this evening and answer his call to you to watch and pray. . . . Spend time with him, as you would have wished to when he was alone in the Garden of Gethsemane. In that sadness allow him to speak to you in the depth of your soul. He alone can help you to understand the meaning of his thirst for you, and how his human love was but the sign of God's love for each of you. Indeed we can say—and thank God for it—he, God, thirsts for you, thirsts for me.

Cardinal Hume, Holy Thursday, 1985

Prayer

God our Father,
at the end of our Lenten journey we enter
into the three holy days
of the Lord's passion, death, and resurrection.
May we glory in the cross of Christ,
for he is our salvation, our life, and our resurrection.

The wisdom of God that restrains the untamed fury of
the waters that are above the firmament, that sets a bridle
on the deep, and keeps back the seas, now pours water
into a basin; and the Master washes the feet of the servants.
The Master who wraps the heaven in clouds girds himself
with a towel; and he in whose hand is the life of all
things kneels down to wash the feet of the servants.

Antiphon from Orthodox Holy Thursday liturgy

Scripture

For I received from the Lord what I also delivered to you,
that the Lord Jesus on the night when he was betrayed
took bread, and when he had given thanks, he broke it,
and said, "This is my body which is for you. Do this in
remembrance of me." In the same way also the cup, after
supper, saying, "This cup is the new covenant in my
blood. Do this, as often as you drink it, in remembrance
of me." For as often as you eat this bread and drink the
cup, you proclaim the Lord's death until he comes.

This is the oldest account of what happened at the Last Supper,
written by St. Paul to the people of Corinth in about AD 54:
1 Corinthians 11:23-26

Good Friday

The cross is a fact in many lives, and most certainly a part of every life at some time. I am now thinking of all those people who have come to me and said: "Why do we have to suffer?"... The questions are all the same—the doubts about God's goodness and love abound. It is natural to feel disturbed. I say to those agonized enquirers that I have no easy answer to give. I share your bewilderment. If I pretended to understand, I would be deceiving you. I cannot do that. But I have not found the full answer to our question. Only God can give you that. But I have had at least a glimpse of the truth. Look at the cross. On it died God-made-man, innocent, sinless, good—he died for a purpose only known fully to God. One day I, too, shall know that purpose. Like much else it is at present hidden from me. But already I see that all death is but a gateway to new life, for Christ who died rose again from the dead. Death has lost its sting. You see the cross and the image of the dying Christ with your eyes; see with the eyes of faith outlined behind the cross the image of the risen Christ. Behind all suffering, seen or experienced, we understand through our faith that from that suffering comes an increase of life in Christ, a promise, too, of everlasting happiness.

Cardinal Hume, Commemoration of the Lord's Passion, Good Friday,
Westminster Cathedral, 1994

Prayer

My song is love unknown,
my Saviour's love to me,
love to the loveless shown,
that they might lovely be.
O, who am I, that for my sake,
my Lord should take frail flesh and die?

Why, what hath my Lord done?
What makes this rage and spite?
He made the lame to run,
he gave the blind their sight.
Sweet injuries! Yet they at these
themselves displease, and 'gainst him rise.

They rise, and needs will have
my dear Lord made away;
a murderer they save,
the Prince of Life they slay.
Yet cheerful he to suff'ring goes,
that he his foes from thence might free.

Samuel Crossman (c. 1624-83), verses 1, 4 and 5

Scripture

Behold, my servant shall prosper; he shall be exalted and lifted up, and shall be very high. As many were astonished at him—his appearance was so marred, beyond human semblance, and his form beyond that of the sons of men— so shall he startle many nations; kings shall shut their mouths because of him; for that which has not been told them they shall see, and that which they have not heard they shall understand. Who has believed what we have heard? And to whom has the arm of the Lord been revealed?

Isaiah 52:13—53:1

The Season of Easter

❧

In the darkness of Holy Saturday evening, a new fire is blessed; a new Easter candle is lit from the flames, and the procession into church begins: "Christ our Light! Thanks be to God!" The Easter Vigil was once the only celebration of the Lord's resurrection, with no service on what is now Easter Sunday morning. Indeed, the Vigil celebration began at sunset and ended at dawn. The Easter Vigil service today takes place on *the* night of all nights, and, in a practice dating back to the early church, new members are often welcomed into the faith and life of the community. It is a chance for all members of the community to renew their faith in the risen Lord. The Easter Vigil is what Lent has been leading up to, and it is the most important feast in the Christian calendar.

Holy Saturday

Tonight's ceremony is rich in symbolism: fire, light, water, and bread and wine. All these are prominent indeed in this celebration, and all are life-giving. We cannot live in the cold without warmth. We cannot survive easily in uninterrupted darkness. Without water we would die, as indeed would be the case if we had neither food nor drink. The cold, darkness, starvation are the enemies of life. Fire, light, water, food, and drink, these are the friends of life.

Tonight we are celebrating life and its victory over death. The life we celebrate is the life we receive at baptism, God's life, divine life, the life that was in him as man. God's life is in us through baptism. That life is fed by the food and drink that Christ has left us—namely his body and blood which we receive in Holy Communion. . . . Maundy Thursday, Good Friday, and Easter live again in every Mass. When we celebrate Mass we receive always the warmth of the Father: love and light and the life of God—Easter's most precious gifts.

Cardinal Hume, Easter Vigil, Westminster Cathedral, 1994

Prayer

What is happening? Today there is a great silence over all the earth, a great silence, and stillness, a great silence because the King sleeps; the earth was in terror and was still, because God slept in the flesh and raised up those who were sleeping from the ages. God has died in the flesh, and the underworld has trembled. . . . The Lord goes in to them holding his victorious weapon, his cross. When Adam, the first created man, sees him, he strikes his breast in terror and calls out to all: "My Lord be with you all." And Christ in reply says to Adam: "And with your spirit." And grasping his hand he raises him up, saying: "Awake, O sleeper, and arise from the dead, and Christ shall give you light."

From an Ancient Homily for Holy Saturday

Scripture

But on the first day of the week, at early dawn, they went
to the tomb, taking the spices which they had prepared.
And they found the stone rolled away from the tomb, but
when they went in they did not find the body. While
they were perplexed about this, behold, two men stood
by them in dazzling apparel; and as they were frightened
and bowed their faces to the ground, the men said to
them, "Why do you seek the living among the dead?
Remember how he told you, while he was still in Galilee,
that the Son of man must be delivered into the hands of
sinful men, and be crucified, and on the third day rise."
And they remembered his words.

*Someone called Luke is mentioned in the New Testament. He was a
medical doctor and a companion of the Apostle Paul. St. Luke's Gospel
is dated sometime between AD 75 and 90: Luke 24:1-8*

Easter Sunday

Death, we are told, has lost its sting; evil has been defeated, and so we sing the kind of refrain throughout this week: "This day was made by the Lord; we rejoice and are glad." But—but—we know, do we not, that the struggle between good and evil will go on, and evil, alas, will often prevail. Death remains about the one certain fact in the lives of each one of us, and there will be suffering, sorrow, and sadness next week as there was last week. Yet we have the audacity to sing: "This day was made by the Lord and we rejoice and are glad." Empty words? Tragic escapism? The unreality of religion? Dope to quiet the people? "This day was made by the Lord and we rejoice and are glad."

The great gift of Easter is hope—Christian hope which makes us have that confidence in God, in his ultimate triumph, and in his goodness and love, which nothing can shake. Christ shared our experience; he suffered as we suffer; he died as we shall die, and for forty days in the desert he underwent the struggle between good and evil. But now it's all different, and whatever the future holds in store, Christian hope gives us inward peace and inward joy. That's what matters.

Cardinal Hume, Easter Sunday, 1983

Prayer

On this day, Lord God,
you opened for us the way to eternal life
through your only Son's victory over death.
Grant that, as we celebrate the feast of his resurrection,
we may be renewed by your Holy Spirit
and rise again in the light of life.

Scripture

O give thanks to the Lord, for he is good;
his steadfast love endures for ever!
Let Israel say, "His steadfast love endures for ever." . . .
Hark, glad songs of victory in the tents of the righteous:
"The right hand of the Lord does valiantly;
the right hand of the Lord is exalted;
the right hand of the Lord does valiantly!"
I shall not die, but I shall live,
and recount the deeds of the Lord. . . .
The stone which the builders rejected
has become the head of the corner.
This is the Lord's doing;
it is marvellous in our eyes.
This is the day which the Lord has made;
let us rejoice and be glad in it.

Psalm 118:1-2, 15-17, 22-24

Easter Week

On Friday last, a small group of Christians gathered
together outside Westminster Central Hall, where
Methodists worship. Anglicans from Westminster Abbey,
and Catholics from this cathedral joined them. What
united us? It was our common faith in the death and
resurrection of Jesus Christ, true God and true man. If we
did not believe this we would not be Christians. If we did
not believe this we would not have been out in the street
in the rain. Not only did we come together to profess our
faith, but we wished to give witness to it, in a sense to
proclaim the great truth. Here was good news which we
wanted to share with others.

Cardinal Hume, Easter Sunday, Westminster Cathedral, 1994

Prayer

Lord God,
you brought us healing through the Easter mysteries.
Continue to be bountiful to your people:
Lead us to the perfect freedom,
by which the joy that gladdens our way on earth
will be fulfilled in heaven
through Christ our Lord.

Scripture

So they departed quickly from the tomb with fear and great joy, and ran to tell his disciples. And behold, Jesus met them and said, "Hail!" And they came up and took hold of his feet and worshipped him. Then Jesus said to them, "Do not be afraid; go and tell my brethren to go to Galilee, and there they will see me."

Matthew 28:8-10

Second Week of Easter

As we walked down Victoria Street a question kept hovering in my mind: How can we tell those passers-by about Jesus Christ? Who he was, what he did, who died and rose from the dead and in so doing enabled us—you and me—to enter into a new life, the culmination of which will be the vision of God. Even now we can look forward to that, the promise of what will be after we have died. How I would like to explain to those passers-by the great significance of Christ's death and resurrection. I could almost read the minds of some of them: "How can a person die and return to life? That is naïve, indeed nonsense." I would then turn to that passer-by and say: "Go and read what St. Paul wrote in a letter to the Corinthians: 'We preach Christ crucified.'" That truth was a stumbling block to some, folly to others. But, to those who are called Christians, the power of God, and the wisdom of God. On another occasion Paul wrote: "If Christ be not risen, then our faith is in vain." I and those others would not have been out on the street in the rain.

Cardinal Hume, Easter Sunday, Westminster Cathedral, 1994

Prayer

Come, my Way, my Truth, my Life:
Such a Way, as gives us breath:
Such a Truth, as ends all strife:
Such a Life, as killeth death.
Come, my Light, my Feast, my Strength:
Such a Light, as shows a feast:
Such a Feast, as mends in length:
Such a Strength, as makes his guest.
Come, my Joy, my Love, my Heart:
Such a Joy, as none can move:
Such a Love, as none can part:
Such a Heart, as joys in love.

George Herbert (1593-1633), "The Call"

Scripture

Now the company of those who believed were of one heart and soul, and no one said that any of the things which he possessed was his own, but they had everything in common. And with great power the apostles gave their testimony to the resurrection of the Lord Jesus, and great grace was upon them all.

The Acts of the Apostles, written by St. Luke between AD 80 and 90, records some of the early missionary activity of the first Christians:
Acts 4:32-33

Third Week of Easter

Peter on one occasion preached to a large crowd about Christ, and told them about his death and resurrection. So convinced were his listeners on that occasion that 3,000 people were baptized on that day, and joined the first Christian communities. What had persuaded those 3,000? It is no mean number. No doubt it was because they had open minds and hearts, so that the Holy Spirit could be at work within them. Their culture had not stifled their religious instinct. That indeed is the problem with ours. No doubt it was the conviction in Peter's voice which was so persuasive.

Cardinal Hume, Easter Sunday, Westminster Cathedral, 1994

Prayer

As we continue to celebrate the resurrection of Jesus Christ,
we pray that God may fill us with the conviction
of the first apostles,
that like them we may proclaim the good news,
that we may witness in the world and bring people
to faith in the risen Lord.

Scripture

And when they had brought them, they set them before
the   council. And the high priest questioned them, saying,
"We strictly charged you not to teach in this name, yet
here you have filled Jerusalem with your teaching, and
you intend to bring this man's blood upon us." But Peter
and the apostles answered, "We must obey God rather
than men. The God of our fathers raised Jesus whom you
killed by hanging him on a tree. God exalted him at his
right hand as Leader and Savior, to give repentance to
Israel and forgiveness of sins. And we are witnesses to
these things, and so is the Holy Spirit whom God has
given to those who obey him. . . ."

They charged the apostles not to speak in the name of
Jesus, and let them go. Then they left the presence of the
council, rejoicing that they were counted worthy to suffer
dishonor for the name. And every day in the temple and
at home they did not cease teaching and preaching Jesus
as the Christ.

Acts 5:27-32, 40b-42

Fourth Week of Easter

We are reminded of perhaps one of the most lovely titles by which our Lord is known. "I am the good shepherd," he said, "my sheep know me and I know them." In the title "shepherd" is contained all that we understand by the care and concern of our blessed Lord for each one of us. We are reminded, too, of his own story about the lost sheep and the ninety-nine he left in order to go in search of that hundredth which was lost. Think of what it must have been to be a shepherd in his day, in that part of the world where the grass is short, water not easy to find, and where sheep are always in danger of being stolen or falling down precipices.

So that title is very precious. Our Lord sees himself as that shepherd leading his flock—as the psalm says: "The Lord is my shepherd, there is nothing I shall want; fresh and green are the pastures where he leads me. . . . "

We must listen to his voice, follow his guidance, and he will lead us through all the problems and difficulties and all the dangers in our daily lives. He leads us finally to those fresh green pastures, which is heaven, and union with God.

Cardinal Hume, Good Shepherd Sunday, April 1994

Prayer

Almighty and ever-living God,
give us new strength
from the courage of Christ our shepherd,
and lead us to join the saints in heaven,
where he lives and reigns with you and the Holy Spirit,
one God, for ever and ever.

Opening Prayer, Fourth Sunday of Easter, Roman Missal

Scripture

Jesus said, "I am the good shepherd. The good shepherd lays
down his life for the sheep. He who is a hireling and not a
shepherd, whose own the sheep are not, sees the wolf
coming and leaves the sheep and flees; and the wolf
snatches them and scatters them. He flees because he is a
hireling and cares nothing for the sheep. I am the good
shepherd; I know my own, and my own know me, as the
Father knows me and I know the Father; and I lay down
my life for the sheep. And I have other sheep, that are not
of this fold; I must bring them also, and they will heed my
voice. So there shall be one flock, one shepherd. For this
reason the Father loves me, because I lay down my life,
that I may take it again. No one takes it from me, but I lay
it down of my own accord. I have power to lay it down,
and I have power to take it again; this charge I have
received from my Father."

John 10:11-18

Fifth Week of Easter

Easter is so much more than a welcome spring holiday. It has its own special meaning and importance. It offers us real hope. It is the key that unlocks the secrets of life. It reveals the immensity of God's love and the future he has planned for each of us. . . . Easter gives us an idea of what our life is for. Through Easter we see how the love of God shines through darkness and discouragement and death. We now have a sure hope that there is a meaning and a purpose in all that happens to us, and a future beyond our wildest dreams.

Cardinal Hume, Easter Sunday Morning, Breakfast Television, 1986

Prayer

God, you sent us your Son to lighten our darkness,
to chase away the shadows of sin.
May our lives be illumined by Jesus,
the Light and Life of the world.

Scripture

My heart is steadfast, O God;
my heart is steadfast!
I will sing and make melody!
Awake, my soul!
Awake, O harp and lyre!
I will awake the dawn!
I will give thanks to thee, O Lord,
among the peoples;
I will sing praises to thee among the nations.
For thy steadfast love is great to the heavens,
thy faithfulness to the clouds.
Be exalted, O God, above the heavens!
Let thy glory be over all the earth!

Psalm 57:7-11

Sixth Week of Easter

Today, perhaps more than any time in our history, the Christian witness is badly needed. If we the baptized Christians do not rise to the occasion, then we fail as Christians to shape society and mould it as God wishes it to be. "Lord, you are our Father; we the clay, you the potter." We can think and pray about that constantly. We are all the work of that potter's hand, who fashions the clay: God our Father, lovingly and with pride, fashioning us.

Cardinal Hume, The Mystery of the Incarnation

Prayer

Father,
we praise you with greater joy than ever
in this Easter season,
when Christ became our paschal sacrifice.
He has made us children of the light,
rising to new and everlasting life.
He has opened the gates of heaven
to receive his faithful people.
His death is our ransom from death:
His resurrection is our rising to life.

Preface of Easter II, Roman Missal

Scripture

In your hearts reverence Christ as Lord. Always be prepared
to make a defence to anyone who calls you to account for
the hope that is in you, yet do it with gentleness and
reverence; and keep your conscience clear, so that, when
you are abused, those who revile your good behaviour in
Christ may be put to shame. For it is better to suffer for
doing right, if that should be God's will, than for doing
wrong. For Christ also died for sins once for all, the
righteous for the unrighteous, that he might bring us to
God, being put to death in the flesh, but made alive in
the spirit.

*The first letter of St. Peter, written sometime between AD 80 and 120,
is an exhortation to holiness of life: 1 Peter 3:15-18*

Seventh Week of Easter

We are brothers and sisters in Christ. We live by the Word he has given us. He is the Word, the Word whom to see is to see the Father, that Word which is the way, the truth, the life. Brothers and sisters in Christ, baptism makes us into one community described as a body, a building, as a vine, as a bride. There is community between us by virtue of our baptism, which it is good to recognize and wonderful to celebrate.

We are pilgrims in the world, a world which is very secular and very materialistic. But we are pilgrims with a mandate, to preach the Word, to bring people to God that they too may be baptized. We are to be one, that the world may believe. But we do not speak with one voice; that is why... we reflect upon and pray for the gift of unity.

Cardinal Hume, Orthodox Vespers, Westminster Cathedral,
January 19, 1997

Prayer

In Christ a new age has dawned;
the long reign of sin is ended;
a broken world has been renewed,
and we are once again made whole.

Preface of Easter IV, Roman Missal

Scripture

Jesus... lifted up his eyes to heaven, and said... "I do not
pray for these only, but also for those who believe in me
through their word, that they may all be one; even as
thou, Father, art in me, and I in thee, that they may also
be in us, so that the world may believe that thou hast
sent me."

John 17:1a, 20-21

Pentecost

The Easter season lasts for fifty days. At the end of that time the church celebrates the feast of Pentecost (from the Greek word *pentekoste*, "fiftieth.") The Jewish feast of Pentecost came at the end of the feast of Weeks, a period of seven weeks from the Passover to the fiftieth day of Pentecost. The Jewish emphasis was on harvest and the first-fruits. The early Christians kept the Jewish feast as a time of thanksgiving and rejoicing. They were celebrating the resurrection, and in this period both fasting and kneeling were forbidden. The Christian feast of Pentecost became associated with the outpouring of the Holy Spirit and was seen as the "birthday" of the church, when, as recounted in the Acts of the Apostles, the followers of Jesus began to go out and continue his mission.

It makes me think, on this Pentecost Sunday, that we are badly in need of a new beginning in our society, a new Pentecost, a change in each one of us, and a change in our society. I often think of those apostles, after the ascension of our Lord, waiting in that upper room prior to the descending of the Holy Spirit; their sense of emptiness, their sense of poverty, deprivation, uncertainty, frailty. And then the Holy Spirit came down upon them and the remarkable transformation took place in them.

Where before they were empty, now they were filled with new zest for the gospel of Christ. Where before they were poor, now they were rich. Where before they were frail, now they were strong. I believe that in our society today the starting point that we need to acknowledge is that we are spiritually poor, by and large. There is a fundamental emptiness. We need to go with great humility and pray that our emptiness be filled, our poverty reversed, and that we be strengthened in our faith.

The Holy Spirit gave the apostles a greater under-standing of their faith, and enabled them to commit themselves to do something about it, and the necessary courage to do so. Those are the gifts we need in our day, a deepening of our faith, the commitment to Christ and his gospel, and the courage to witness.

Cardinal Hume, Evensong Pentecost Sunday, Great Hormead,
June 7, 1992

Prayer

At creation, the Spirit hovered over the waters;
at Pentecost the Spirit hovered over those in the
    upper room,
dispelling their fear and filling them with courage
to continue the work of Jesus.
May we, too, be open to that Spirit of Jesus,
that we may continue his mission.

Scripture

When the day of Pentecost had come, they were all
together in one place. And suddenly a sound came from
heaven like the rush of a mighty wind, and it filled all the
house where they were sitting. And there appeared to
them tongues as of fire, distributed and resting on each
one of them. And they were all filled with the Holy Spirit
and began to speak in other tongues, as the Spirit gave
them utterance.

Acts 2:1-4

The Season of Quiet Reflection

∽

The church's year is, in many respects, one long opportunity for reflection and celebration. The great feast of Easter and the celebration of Jesus' birth at Christmas are the high points of that year. In comparison, the rest of the year can seem somewhat ordinary. In fact, the church's year between Easter and the start of preparations for Christmas is actually called "Ordinary Time." This is not to say that that time of year is less important. Rather than concentrating on particular feasts, it can be an opportunity for reflection on many important themes and questions in our journey towards the Father.

Stillness and Peace

Allow me to think and dream in your presence, and in so doing to speak to you of that which I believe is the purpose of all academic endeavor.

I shall speak of thoughts which come when alone, uncluttered by the immediate, free from pressure, reflecting in the cool of the evening after the heat of the day. How difficult it is to make space to be silent and to find solitude to be still, and yet it is in silence and stillness that we hear the voice of God calling us to look for him in the world he has created and to listen to his speaking deep within. God is not in the hurricane, nor in the earthquake, nor in the fire, but in the sound of stillness (1 Kings 19).

To be silent and still is an art to be learned. It has its own discipline and difficulties, but the learning of it is essential, lest we be trapped in the purely secular and the material, escaping from the emptiness of the former by indulging in the attractions of the latter. True religion does not condemn what is material, nor does it fail to respect the laws of science, economics, medicine. It teaches that this world is good, that we are stewards of creation, and in cultivating its riches we work with the Creator, and ourselves grow—but a steward so easily becomes an exploiter and the perfection of the individual an end in itself. We have to withdraw from time to time to be silent and still— to get perspective, to look beyond this world and to search for the origin and purpose of all. . . .

Be silent and still; look and listen; then, as St. Paul
wrote to the Romans, from things visible we come to the
knowledge of the one who is beyond the experiences of
our senses. "Ever since the creation of the world his
everlasting power and deity, however invisible, have been
there for the mind to see in the things he has made"
(Romans 1:20).

That is a profound truth.

*Cardinal Hume, Honorary Degree Ceremony, London,
February 6, 1999*

Prayer

Drop thy still dews of quietness,
    Till all our strivings cease;
Take from our souls the strain and stress,
And let our ordered lives confess
    The beauty of thy peace.

Breathe through the heats of our desire
    Thy coolness and thy balm;
Let sense be dumb; let flesh retire;
Speak through the earthquake, wind, and fire,
    O still, small voice of calm!

*John Greenleaf Whittier (1807-92),
from "The Brewing of Soma"*

Scripture

For God alone my soul waits in silence;
from him comes my salvation.
He only is my rock and my salvation,
my fortress; I shall not be greatly moved.

How long will you set upon a man
to shatter him, all of you,
like a leaning wall, a tottering fence?
They only plan to thrust him down from
     his eminence.
They take pleasure in falsehood.
They bless with their mouths,
but inwardly they curse.

For God alone my soul waits in silence,
for my hope is from him.
He only is my rock and my salvation,
my fortress; I shall not be shaken.
On God rests my deliverance and my honor;
my mighty rock, my refuge, is God.

Trust in him at all times, O people;
pour out your heart before him;
God is a refuge for us.

Psalm 62:1-8

Prayer

When you get no consolation in prayer, when you feel
you are getting nowhere, that may be the best prayer you
have ever said, because you are doing it not for your sake,
but for God's. Always seek the God of consolation; never
seek the consolations of God. It is always that way round.

Quite often we are in a kind of distraught mood, and
simply don't know how to pray, feeling that deep sense of
being lost. It is good at such times to see oneself rather
like the lost sheep in the parable caught in the briars,
surrounded by fog; the more you try to escape from the
brambles the more you get entangled. The more you try
to rush through the fog the more likely you are to get
lost. When you are in that mood just wait in your prayer,
wait for him to come and disentangle you.

Cardinal Hume, The Mystery of Love

Prayer

Ever-listening God,
give me the faith to trust in you,
the patience to listen to you
and not tell you what I think you should do.
Help me to pray the words,
"Your will be done on earth as it is in heaven;"
and having prayed this way,
may I accept your will.

Scripture

And when you pray, you must not be like the hypocrites; for they love to stand and pray in the synagogues and at the street corners, that they may be seen by men. Truly, I say to you, they have received their reward. But when you pray, go into your room and shut the door and pray to your Father who is in secret; and your Father who sees in secret will reward you.

And in praying do not heap up empty phrases as the Gentiles do; for they think that they will be heard for their many words. Do not be like them, for your Father knows what you need before you ask him. Pray then like this:

> Our Father who art in heaven,
> Hallowed be thy name.
> Thy kingdom come,
> Thy will be done,
>   On earth as it is in heaven.
> Give us this day our daily bread;
> And forgive us our debts,
>   As we also have forgiven our debtors;
> And lead us not into temptation,
>   But deliver us from evil.

Matthew 6:5-13

Longing for God

Be silent and still, and look also inwards, first at the darkness within, at conflicting emotions, at the emptiness of the heart, at inner wounds. We are in need of healing, or nearly always so, and in need too of being saved from what is base and ignoble. Whence come those lustful thoughts, involuntary angers, shameful jealousies. We are not as we should be. When silent and still we can, I believe, hear his voice speaking to us through our weakness and inadequacy, coaxing our minds to look for one who will bring order into that inner chaos, but most of all to give forgiveness and encouragement. He speaks too through anguish and agony to draw us away from what separates us from him to look to him for serenity and inner peace.

There is also light within, our desires and longings, our aspirations to rise above what is of this world, to discover the perfection of love and a happiness we can never lose. Such happiness, and the love that is its secret, elude us however much we may relish a foretaste of them in our present experience or delight in the hints they gave of a future bliss. We long to escape from the darkness that we may dwell forever in the light. Our longing is, ultimately, for what we cannot now have. It will be satisfied only by what is, at the present, beyond our reach. Happiness, complete and unending, is for later, not now. Restless hearts will ache no more when in possession of the absolute good.

Is there one with power to heal? Is there a teacher who will speak to me of truths that my mind cannot discover? Where is the guide to show me the way through life's problems and difficulties?

The Christian knows that there is such a one. It is he who spoke of himself as the way, the truth and the life. . . .

Stand back from time to time; then take your eye off the immediate, and dream about the ultimate, about the absolute, about God.

*Cardinal Hume, Honorary Degree Ceremony, London,
February 6, 1999*

Prayer

Dear God,
we long to be with you,
to be in your presence.
In this pilgrimage on earth
may we never lose sight of you
and draw ever closer to you.
Give us the strength each day
to stand back and dedicate some time
solely to you.

Scripture

As a hart longs for flowing streams,
so longs my soul for thee, O God.
My soul thirsts for God, for the living God.
When shall I come and behold the face of God?
My tears have been my food day and night,
while men say to me continually,
"Where is your God?"

These things I remember,
as I pour out my soul:
how I went with the throng,
and led them in procession to the house of God,
with glad shouts and songs of thanksgiving,
a multitude keeping festival.
Why are you cast down, O my soul,
and why are you disquieted within me?
Hope in God; for I shall again praise him,
my help and my God.

Oh send out thy light and thy truth;
let them lead me;
let them bring me to thy holy hill
and to thy dwelling!
Then I will go to the altar of God,
to God my exceeding joy;
and I will praise thee with the lyre,
O God, my God.

Psalm 42:1-5; 43:3-4

Worship of God

"So long as you eat this bread and drink this cup you proclaim the Lord's death until he comes" (1 Corinthians 11:26). Those wonderful words on which the church has meditated down the ages have made the Eucharist the very center of our lives. Today on this feast of the body and blood of Christ we do well to profess our faith again in the reality of the presence of Christ's body in the consecrated host and his blood in the consecrated wine.

The Council of Trent [1545-63] spoke about that wonderful change, and it is very awesome to think that at the very words of the priest standing at the altar—speaking those same words—the bread becomes his body and the wine his blood, and in doing so, gives us the possibility of re-enacting the sacrifice of Calvary and of receiving Christ in Holy Communion, to be closely united to him. For these two gifts: the sacrifice of Calvary and his coming to us in that intimate way, we give thanks today in reaffirming our faith as I have suggested.

St. Paul in that very same passage went on to write: "Whoever eats the bread or drinks the cup of the Lord in an unworthy manner will be guilty of profaning the body and blood of the Lord. So it is with pure motives that we must approach him, with humility, and with our desire to please him, and do his will."

Our danger is always, of course, that we become so familiar with our going to Holy Communion that the enormity and awesomeness of it we begin to take too much for granted.

So as we celebrate this feast we have an opportunity to pause and reflect on exactly what we are doing and what is implied.

Cardinal Hume, Feast of Corpus Christi, Westminster Cathedral,
May 27, 1997

Prayer

We praise and worship you, God our creator.
You have created us in your image,
though we are unworthy.
You have given us your Son,
who continues to nourish us
through the gift of his body and blood.
May we never be separated from you,
and may our worship be worthy of you,
God our life-giver.

Scripture

For I received from the Lord what I also delivered to you,
that the Lord Jesus on the night when he was betrayed
took bread, and when he had given thanks, he broke it,
and said, "This is my body which is for you. Do this in
remembrance of me." In the same way also the cup, after
supper, saying, "This cup is the new covenant in my
blood. Do this, as often as you drink it, in remembrance
of me." For as often as you eat this bread and drink the
cup, you proclaim the Lord's death until he comes.

Whoever, therefore, eats the bread or drinks the cup of
the Lord in an unworthy manner will be guilty of profaning
the body and blood of the Lord. Let a man examine
himself, and so eat of the bread and drink of the cup. For
any one who eats and drinks without discerning the body
eats and drinks judgment upon himself.

1 Corinthians 11:23-29

God's Call

There is a very clear and close connection between the sacrament of confirmation and the work of evangelizing. . . . Confirmation, like baptism, is given only once, but it is a constant source of grace making us sensitive instruments of the work of the Holy Spirit. When we were baptized we became followers of Christ, disciples learning from him, and we were consecrated to the Father as he, Jesus Christ, was consecrated.

Our responsibility as baptized Christians was to acknowledge and profess our faith and grow in our knowledge and in our appreciation of it. Confirmation completes the sacrament of baptism. We can say that just as baptism consecrated us to God, so in a sense confirmation dedicates us to a special way of following Christ. We become co-workers, co-operators, in order to achieve the work of Christ in the world...

A Christian is automatically, instinctively, a missioner— because instinctively he should want, she should want, to communicate what he or she has received. You remember how when the Holy Spirit came down upon the apostles there was a mood of excitement, almost irresponsible excitement, as Peter, John, and the other apostles spoke of the things Jesus Christ had done. Wouldn't it be a wonderful thing if all of you in this cathedral today, allowing the grace of your confirmation to be renewed, went out excited and enthusiastic to tell others that God is love and that from that simple fact everything else follows.

You may say, my vocation is to remain at home; my vocation is to do my job in this country, in this city. But if you remain where you are in your vocation, you still remain a missioner—in the home, in the family, and at work. And make no mistake about it, this too—our own country—has become a mission land; the gospel has to be preached, as it were, all over again. There is a sense in which we have to begin all over again, because so many have fallen away, because so many today in this city have not heard the good news. There is a spiritual vacuum to be filled; and who is going to fill it unless it is you, the people of God.

Cardinal Hume, Westminster Cathedral, October 14, 1979

Prayer

All-powerful God,
help me to listen for the sound of your voice.
May I answer when you call,
responding eagerly to do your will
and proclaim your good news.

Scripture

And there [on Mount Horeb] Elijah came to a cave, and lodged there; and behold, the word of the Lord came to him, and he said to him, "What are you doing here, Elijah?" He said, "I have been very jealous for the Lord, the God of hosts; for the people of Israel have forsaken thy covenant, thrown down thy altars, and slain thy prophets with the sword; and I, even I only, am left; and they seek my life, to take it away." And he said, "Go forth, and stand upon the mount before the Lord." And behold, the Lord passed by, and a great and strong wind rent the mountains, and broke in pieces the rocks before the Lord, but the Lord was not in the wind; and after the wind an earthquake, but the Lord was not in the earthquake; and after the earthquake a fire, but the Lord was not in the fire; and after the fire a still small voice. And when Elijah heard it, he wrapped his face in his mantle and went out and stood at the entrance of the cave.

The books of the Kings were probably written during the exile of the Jewish people in Babylon (586-538 BC) recounting the stories of some of the people's rulers: 1 Kings 19:9-13a

Love of God
and Love of Neighbor

That commandment to love God is clear, and we are
furthermore expected to put our whole selves into it. It is
easy enough to give notional assent to this proposition,
but real assent, translated into a program of action, is
quite another thing. And in any case we can see our
neighbor, but how can we love someone whom we do
not see? The answer is given by St. John in his first letter
when he writes that it all starts with our realizing that
God loves us first. When that becomes clear, then we
begin to want to love God in return. . . .

[Furthermore] we have to try to discover what is
good and lovable in all those with whom we come in
contact. It is only thus that we shall come to see them
as God sees them, for each one of us is made in the
image and likeness of God. So the more we approach
others with sympathy and concern the more our eyes
are opened to see God in them. In this way our attempts
to get our relationships right with others should lead us
to a greater love of God. Such an approach makes heavy
demands on us.

All the time I'm speaking there is ringing in my mind
another demand of the Lord, and it is succinct and clear:
"Be ye perfect as your heavenly Father is perfect." It
means that if we are to love God and our neighbor, then
we must be constantly changing, because we do not,

and we never will, function as we should. We belong to
a fallen race; we get it wrong too often. Pride and
self-centeredness ruin not only the lives of others, but
our own too. So, I see this present life as a period of
training, a time of preparation during which we learn
the art of loving God and our neighbor; sometimes
succeeding, sometimes failing, but convinced that the
ultimate purpose of our life is the love of God and
neighbor.

Cardinal Hume, Lent Talk, March 1979

Prayer

O my God, I am truly sorry for all my sins.
Your Son Jesus reminded us how important it is
to love you and to love our neighbor.
I am sorry for not loving you and not loving others.
Help me to live like Jesus.

Scripture

But when the Pharisees heard that he had silenced the
Sadducees, they came together. And one of them, a lawyer,
asked him a question, to test him. "Teacher, which is the great
commandment in the law?" And he said to him, "You shall love
the Lord your God with all your heart, and with all your soul,
and with all your mind. This is the great and first commandment.
And a second is like it, You shall love your neighbor as yourself.
On these two commandments depend all the law and the
prophets."

Matthew 22:34-40

Friendship and Love

A well-known Archbishop of Canterbury, and one much respected, once said that there is a space within each person which only God can fill. It is a saying that I have always found to be helpful, and important. That space within me is waiting for God; if I do not admit him into my life, then there will always be an emptiness within me, a void.

You may wonder about that space within you, as I do about mine within me. But I find consolation in this thought: There was no room for him in the inn, so it was in a stable—a cave hewn out of the rock on the side of a hill—that Jesus came into this world. Could any place be more unsuitable or unpromising than this? So take heart. Your space may seem to you to be unsuitable; certainly unpromising. He does, however, wish and choose to occupy that space within you.

How do I understand that coming of him into that space? I believe that it is the language of friendship or love which will help us to do so. God wants to dwell in our thoughts. He wants to have a place in our affections. Two lovers thinking about each other; two lovers wanting each other: There is a good starting point for our reflection.

Cardinal Hume, Midnight Mass, Westminster Cathedral, 1997

Prayer

All-loving God,
you call us to be your friends.
May we open our hearts to you,
that you may fill us with your love.
May we carry your love within us
wherever we go,
for you are with us always.
And may we share that love with others.

Scripture

For God so loved the world that he gave his only Son,
that   whoever believes in him should not perish but
have eternal life. For God sent the Son into the world,
not to condemn the world, but that the world might be
saved through him. . . . He who does what is true comes
to the light, that it may be clearly seen that his deeds
have been wrought in God.

John 3:16-17, 21

Loneliness

It is my life's experience that there is no day on which I shall keep from tears and not know sadness or misfortune. I weep bitter tears for myself when my mind knows only anguish and anxiety, my body pain and fatigue. If God be the goodness which is claimed for him, if he has that love for us which no human love can match, then why does evil seem to rule our hearts and hold sway in his creation? Yet his message is still, "Rejoice, do not be afraid."

Terror comes when we see no escape from the darkness that surrounds us, when we see no light. Terror is the child of despair, ugly and cruel. But when terror holds us in its grip, hope is often born. Darkness yields to light. A Savior has been born, the Lord Christ himself. . . .

"Do not be afraid." We need never be alone; every burden carried by us is also shared by him. "Give me your burden," he says, "and I will make it mine." He will not always lift the burden from us, but being his too, it is lighter now and sweeter. We do not understand why we are fallen and sinful, burdened and wounded. He does not will our sadness or our pain. He wants us to know his goodness and to trust, to find his love and rejoice. The secret hidden in his words will slowly be shown to us. It is the secret of his love; warm, close, and true.

Cardinal Hume, Christmas Meditation, 1982

Prayer

Dear God, be with those
who feel lonely and unloved.
May they feel enveloped
by the warmth of your Spirit.
May they know your presence,
respond to your love,
and realize your closeness to them
    at all times.
And when I am lonely,
be with me, too.

Scripture

O Lord, rebuke me not in thy anger,
nor chasten me in thy wrath.
Be gracious to me, O Lord, for I am languishing;
O Lord, heal me, for my bones are troubled.
My soul also is sorely troubled.
But thou, O Lord—how long?

Turn, O Lord; save my life;
deliver me for the sake of thy steadfast love.
For in death there is no remembrance of thee;
in Sheol who can give thee praise?

I am weary with my moaning;
every night I flood my bed with tears;
I drench my couch with my weeping.
My eye wastes away because of grief;
it grows weak because of all my foes.

Depart from me, all you workers of evil;
for the Lord has heard the sound of my weeping.
The Lord has heard my supplication;
the Lord accepts my prayer.

Psalm 6:1-9

Holiness

This feast of All Saints in a marvellous way affects all our families. Those persons who through the fidelity of their lives, the living out of their state of life, responding to their vocation, are now receiving their reward. . . .

Anonymous saints, but all nonetheless saints. And they became holy in no dramatic manner, by no great deeds of heroism, but using the ordinary things of everyday life—at home, at work, at recreation, striving in every action they did, in every attitude which they had, to do the will of God; because holiness consists in this, the doing of the will of God. It consists in learning to turn the ordinary humdrum things of life into acts of love; the will of God done and loved in everyday acts, in what we do, in what we suffer. The formula is tolerably easy to understand but the doing of it remarkably difficult. It is a life's work to learn to live in conformity with the will of God. And what is the secret of knowing what the will of God is and the receiving of the strength to do it? It comes from a life of prayer, because it is in prayer and through prayer that we become attuned, as it were, to the things of God, and when so attuned have that instinct of what it is that pleases him and the courage to carry it out.

One day we shall be "All Saints," and those who come after us will be, please God, celebrating this feast remembering you and me, anonymous and unknown, but precious in the eyes of God.

Cardinal Hume, Feast of All Saints, 1985

Prayer

God, our holy Father,
you have given us an example to follow
in Jesus, your Son.
May our lives be holy,
as we show our belief in you,
in all that we say, and think, and do.

Scripture

Seeing the crowds, he went up on the mountain, and when he sat down his disciples came to him. And he opened his mouth and taught them, saying:

"Blessed are the poor in spirit, for theirs is the kingdom of heaven.

"Blessed are those who mourn, for they shall be comforted.

"Blessed are the meek, for they shall inherit the earth.

"Blessed are those who hunger and thirst for righteousness, for they shall be satisfied.

"Blessed are the merciful, for they shall obtain mercy.

"Blessed are the pure in heart, for they shall see God.

"Blessed are the peacemakers, for they shall be called sons of God.

"Blessed are those who are persecuted for righteousness' sake, for theirs is the kingdom of heaven.

"Blessed are you when men revile you and persecute you and utter all kinds of evil against you falsely on my account. Rejoice and be glad, for your reward is great in heaven, for so men persecuted the prophets who were before you."

Matthew 5:1-12

Suffering

There is no clear certain answer to the question, "Why?" which will run through our heads. Where do we go, then, to find some suggestion where the answer may be? If not, where do we go to find some comfort? St. Paul, writing to the Romans, reminds us: "For I am sure that neither death, nor life, nor angels, nor principalities, nor things present, nor things to come, nor powers, nor height, nor depth, nor anything else in all creation, will be able to separate us from the love of God in Christ Jesus our Lord" (Romans 8:38-39).

There is a phrase "blind faith"—blind because we do not see clearly, faith because we have to take the faith of another. That word of St. Paul is, I believe, the only one that can give true comfort. We do not understand, yet cannot and must not doubt, that there is some meaning in the providence of God which is hidden from us. If we speak of the providence of God there will always be that element of love which will be the ultimate explanation of why we weep, why we suffer. Hang on to that one simple truth, that somehow in the providence of God his love will be in action.

Cardinal Hume, Mass for Honduras Victims, Westminster Cathedral, November 27, 1998

Prayer

Father,
your Son accepted our sufferings
to teach us the virtue of patience in human illness.
Hear the prayers we offer for our sick brothers and sisters.
May all who suffer pain, illness or disease...
know that they are joined to Christ
in his suffering for the salvation of the world,
who lives and reigns with you and the Holy Spirit,
one God, for ever and ever.

Opening Prayer of Mass for the Sick, Roman Missal

Scripture

Hear my prayer, O Lord;
let my cry come to thee!
Do not hide thy face from me
in the day of my distress!
Incline thy ear to me;
answer me speedily in the day when I call!

For my days pass away like smoke,
and my bones burn like a furnace.
My heart is smitten like grass, and withered;
I forget to eat my bread.
Because of my loud groaning
my bones cleave to my flesh.
I am like a vulture of the wilderness,
like an owl of the waste places...
My days are like an evening shadow;
I wither away like grass.

But thou, O Lord, art enthroned for ever;
thy name endures to all generations.
Thou wilt arise and have pity on Zion;
it is the time to favor her;
the appointed time has come.
For thy servants hold her stones dear,
and have pity on her dust. . . .
For the Lord will build up Zion;
he will appear in his glory;
he will regard the prayer of the destitute,
and will not despise their supplication.

Psalm 102:1-6, 11-14, 16-17

Death

We ask why, why?
We did so at Dunblane and at Aberfan.
We do so now on the death of Diana, Princess of Wales.
Death is a formidable foe until we learn to make it a friend.
Death is to be feared if we do not learn to welcome it.
Death is the ultimate absurdity if we do not see it as fulfilment.
Death haunts us when viewed as a journey into nothingness
rather than a pilgrimage to a place where true happiness is
    to be found.
The human mind cannot understand death.
We face it with fear and uncertainty, revulsion even;
or we turn away from the thought, for it is too hard to bear.
But faith gives answers when reason fails.
The strong instinct to live points to immortality.
Faith admits us into death's secrets.
Death is not the end of the road, but a gateway to a better
    place.
It is in this place that our noblest aspirations will be realized.
It is here that we will understand how our experiences of
    goodness, love, beauty, and joy
are realities which exist perfectly in God.
It is in heaven that we shall rest in him,
    and our hearts will be restless
until they rest in God.

We, left to continue our pilgrimage through life, weep and
mourn.
Sadness reigns in our hearts.
You, Diana, and your companions too, are on your way to
union with him
who loves you so.
He knows the love which you, Diana, had for others.
God speaks now of his love for you.
Our tears will not be bitter ones now but a gentle weeping
to rob our sadness of its agony
and lead at last to peace,
peace with God.

Cardinal Hume, a reflection following the death of Diana,
Princess of Wales, in August 1997

Prayer

Father, all-powerful and ever-living God,
we do well always and everywhere to give you thanks
through Jesus Christ our Lord.
In him, who rose from the dead,
our hope of resurrection dawned.
The sadness of death gives way
to the bright promise of immortality.
Lord, for your faithful people life is changed, not ended.
When the body of our earthly dwelling lies in death,
we gain an everlasting dwelling place in heaven.

Preface of Christian Death I, Roman Missal

Scripture

Out of the depths I cry to thee, O Lord!
Lord, hear my voice!
Let thy ears be attentive
to the voice of my supplications!

If thou, O Lord, shouldst mark iniquities,
Lord, who could stand?
But there is forgiveness with thee,
that thou mayest be feared.

I wait for the Lord; my soul waits,
and in his word I hope;
my soul waits for the Lord
more than watchmen for the morning,
more than watchmen for the morning.

O Israel, hope in the Lord!
For with the Lord there is steadfast love,
and with him is plenteous redemption.
And he will redeem Israel from all his iniquities.

Psalm 130

Vision of God

On another occasion the Apostle Thomas asked our Lord: "Lord, we do not know where you are going; how can we know the way?" (John 14:5) and he answered: "I am the way, and the truth, and the life." If you want the truth about who we are, what we are destined for, it is Jesus Christ who teaches us. If you want to know the way to travel through this world and have a future in the next, he is the way. If you want to be filled with his life, it is from him that we receive it.

That opens up for us what we are all destined for, or indeed made for, which is after death to enjoy the vision of God face to face. That experience will be the total fulfilment of all that we desired in this life, all the best for which we aimed.

It is sad that there are so many people who simply do not know what lies before them after death: a moment of ecstatic love which will never cease and of which we can never be deprived. That is a wonderful thought and one which consoles us so much when we have lost a close relative, lost a dear friend, lost a colleague, as so many of us . . . have experienced.

In our Catholic tradition we pray for the dead. Why? Because to approach God, to be in the presence of God, will be very awesome, and inevitably we shall feel inadequate, unworthy. I for one rejoice in our teaching about purgatory where we can be finally prepared for the vision of God. . . .

That is our belief, and that is what we are doing . . .
praying for those who await their final journey into
heaven. . . .

Cardinal Hume, Catholic Police Guild Requiem Mass, November 1998

Prayer

All-powerful God,
you have called us to be with you in heaven.
May our lives here on earth
be true preparation for the journey
to our longed-for home in heaven,
where we will see you face to face
and be at peace in your presence for ever.

Scripture

On this mountain the Lord of hosts will make for all peoples a feast of fat things, a feast of wine on the lees, of fat things full of marrow, of wine on the lees well refined. And he will destroy on this mountain the covering that is cast over all peoples, the veil that is spread over all nations. He will swallow up death for ever, and the Lord God will wipe away tears from all faces, and the reproach of his people he will take away from all the earth; for the Lord has spoken.

It will be said on that day, "Lo, this is our God; we have waited for him, that he might save us. This is the Lord; we have waited for him; let us be glad and rejoice in his salvation."

Isaiah 25:6-9

The Season of Advent

◆

Towards the end of the year the church concentrates minds and hearts once again on specific themes as it celebrates the season of Advent, a time of preparation. It has been known for the earliest Christmas cards and gifts to go on sale in the middle of the summer, almost four months before Christmas Day itself. The countdown of the number of shopping days left begins and the great season of "spend, spend, spend" comes into full swing. But the true preparation for what Christmas is really about begins on the First Sunday of Advent.

Advent, from the Latin *adventus*, "coming," is a season of preparation for the coming of Jesus. Like Lent, Advent has no meaning on its own but is purely a time of preparation. Advent seems to have evolved as some sort of penitential season, a time of fasting before the feasting of Christmas. By the sixth century, there was a four-week preparation period, the Advent season.

One of the Advent themes was clearly penitential. Here the emphasis was not just in celebrating the coming of Jesus into the world, but also his final coming in judgment. Today this theme is continued with the call to conversion made by St. John the Baptist, the forerunner of Jesus. Towards the end of the four-week season of Advent the focus shifts to the imminent celebration of the coming of Jesus, the Word made flesh.

First Week of Advent

[On the First Sunday of Advent] we shall be thinking of the words of our Lord, quoted by St. Mark, "the kingdom of God is at hand; repent, and believe in the gospel" (Mark 1:15). Our Lord is telling us to have a change of heart and to listen to his word, and to accept it. I suggest that throughout Advent you pay special attention to the words, "thy kingdom come," when you recite the Our Father. Ponder on them and ask the Holy Spirit to help you understand the meaning of those words and their implications for you. He will then rule within us, not like a king in a palace, but as a child born in a stable; not as one wielding power and inspiring fear, but as a shepherd leading us, you and me—so often wayward, sometimes a bit lost—to a place where there will be no more tears; there will be no more death, and no more mourning and sadness (Revelation 21:4).

Cardinal Hume, Pastoral Letter, Feast of Christ the King, 1986

Prayer

Let us pray that we may take Christ's coming seriously.
All-powerful God,
increase our strength of will for doing good
that Christ may find an eager welcome at his coming
and call us to his side in the kingdom of heaven
where he lives and reigns with you and the Holy Spirit,
one God, for ever and ever.

Opening Prayer, First Sunday of Advent, Roman Missal

Scripture

The word which Isaiah the son of Amoz saw concerning
Judah and Jerusalem.

It shall come to pass in the latter days
that the mountain of the house of the Lord
shall be established as the highest of the mountains,
and shall be raised above the hills;
and all the nations shall flow to it,
and many peoples shall come, and say:
"Come, let us go up to the mountain of the Lord,
to the house of the God of Jacob;
that he may teach us his ways
and that we may walk in his paths."
For out of Zion shall go forth the law,
and the word of the Lord from Jerusalem.
He shall judge between the nations,
and shall decide for many peoples;
and they shall beat their swords into ploughshares,
and their spears into pruning hooks;
nation shall not lift up sword against nation,
neither shall they learn war any more.

O house of Jacob,
come, let us walk
in the light of the Lord.

Isaiah 2:1-5

Second Week of Advent

What must we do then for Advent? May I suggest two things, two small but practical possibilities to ensure that our time of preparation for the coming of Christ at Christmas is well spent.

During Advent, begin your day as you open your eyes with the words: "Praised be Jesus Christ." These four words can focus your waking thoughts on God's presence, on his love for you. If, even for a fleeting moment, you turn to him with love right at the beginning of the day, you will have begun it in the very best possible way. Do the same last thing at night. Try to make an awareness of his presence your last waking thought. If you do that, then you will have put your day into context. From start to finish it is lived in God's presence. Thinking about God in this way gradually makes us one with him and gives us that inner peace which is so precious.

My second suggestion is that you seek an opportunity during the season of Advent to show forgiveness. Christmas is a time of reconciliation—God became man so that the rift between him and us caused by sin should be healed. Christmas is quite rightly a time for family and friends, but we know too well how even the closest family suffers from tension and sometimes from grudges. Sometimes friends misunderstand each other; offence is taken. Your peace of mind might even now be spoilt by a refusal to forgive someone who has injured you. Be forgiving. The first step can be hard. It requires humility. Forgiveness reconciles us with one another, and so brings peace into the family or with the community in which we live.

Cardinal Hume, Advent Pastoral Letter, 1982

Prayer

Let us pray that nothing may hinder us
from receiving Christ with joy.
God of power and mercy,
open our hearts in welcome.
Remove the things that hinder us
from receiving Christ with joy,
so that we may share his wisdom
and become one with him
when he comes in glory.

Opening Prayer, Second Sunday of Advent, Roman Missal

Scripture

The beginning of the gospel of Jesus Christ, the Son of God.
As it is written in Isaiah the prophet,

"Behold, I send my messenger before thy face,
who shall prepare thy way;
the voice of one crying in the wilderness:
Prepare the way of the Lord,
make his paths straight—"

John the baptizer appeared in the wilderness, preaching a baptism of repentance for the forgiveness of sins. . . . Now John was clothed with camel's hair, and had a leather girdle around his waist, and ate locusts and wild honey. And he preached, saying, "After me comes he who is mightier than I, the thong of whose sandals I am not worthy to stoop down and untie. I have baptized you with water; but he will baptize you with the Holy Spirit."

St. Mark's Gospel was the first to be written, shortly after the persecution of Christians by the Emperor Nero. He blamed them for the burning of the city of Rome in AD 64: Mark 1:1-4, 6-8

Third Week of Advent

Words—like looking forward, expectation, hope—are the ones that come to mind as I think of the season of Advent. We look forward—we look forward to Christmas, to celebrate that great feast, and in the liturgy we make our own the thoughts and the mood of those who were awaiting the Messiah. But the church is looking forward too, to that mysterious moment in time when the end of the world will come, and Christ will appear in all his glory. When that moment will be, and how exactly it will come about, we do not know. Meanwhile, with mounting excitement, we approach the feast of Christmas—the four weeks of preparation are to enable us to celebrate worthily, so we can renew on that day that great act of faith which enables us to profess and confess that the Second Person of the Blessed Trinity became man and dwelt amongst us; and we want to celebrate by praising and thanking God for all that that great Mystery means and has done for us. . . .

It seems to me that the feast of Advent is the feast of hope, Christian hope, which includes within it not only a looking forward to a time when all will be well, but an unshakeable confidence that, in the providence of God, things will work out in our own lives as well. We look forward to the great feast of Christmas to strengthen our faith in the presence of God among us made man, because we know that it is in that fact that the salvation of the world will come.

Cardinal Hume, Advent Pastoral Letter, 1977

Prayer

Come to us, Lord Jesus Christ,
come as we search the scriptures
and see God's hidden purpose,
come as we walk the lonely road,
needing a companion,
come when life mystifies and perplexes us,
come into our disappointments and unease,
come at table when we share our food and hopes,
and, coming, open our eyes to recognize you.

Donald Hilton (b. 1932), "Come, Lord Jesus"

Scripture

Now when John heard in prison about the deeds of the Christ, he sent word by his disciples and said to him, "Are you he who is to come, or shall we look for another?" And Jesus answered them, "Go and tell John what you hear and see: the blind receive their sight and the lame walk, lepers are cleansed and the deaf hear, and the dead are raised up, and the poor have good news preached to them. And blessed is he who takes no offense at me."

Matthew 11:2-6

Fourth Week of Advent

"She conceived by the power of the Holy Spirit": astonishing words, just the fact that God entered into our world and became man. Mary was chosen to be the mother. She conceived miraculously. It is hard just to reflect and take in the impact which those facts should have upon us. They are so familiar that we cease to advert to them. Or perhaps we have been influenced by those who ridicule such thoughts.

It could not happen, to be conceived miraculously, so it did not happen, they will say.

It did. She conceived by the power of the Holy Spirit. That is the faith which we profess on this day. The incarnation began at that moment. What was conceived was human life, the human life of Jesus. It is right and proper that we should have our thoughts today on . . . the celebration of his birth.

Open up the door of your heart for he is knocking and we are free to say "Come in" or not. Mary allowed him into her life, and in a unique manner, because she became his mother.

There may be many, too many, who shut God out of their lives and say "No" when he knocks. He himself is a generous host; he opens his door to us, always ready to welcome us, and when we enter his world he has gifts, priceless gifts, for each one of us. . . .

Whichever way we think about it, either the door of your heart and your cry to him to come in, or whether

you think of his door inviting us, welcoming us to enter
into his abode, Mary is always an example, because she
welcomed him into her life with those words: "Be it done
unto me according to thy word." Her fiat, her saying yes
to God, brought her Son—his Son—into our world.

So this is a day to deepen our faith in the fact that
Jesus Christ, true God and true man, was conceived by
the power of the Holy Spirit.

Cardinal Hume, Feast of the Annunciation,
Westminster Cathedral, March 25, 1999

Prayer

Maiden, yet a mother,
daughter of thy Son,
high beyond all other,
lowlier is none;
thou the consummation
planned by God's decree,
when our lost creation
nobler rose in thee.

Thus his place prepared,
he who all things made
'mid his creatures tarried,
in thy bosom laid;
there his love he nourished,
warmth that gave increase
to the root whence flourished
our eternal peace.

Lady, lest our vision,
striving heavenward, fail,
still let thy petition
with thy Son prevail,
unto whom all merit,
power and majesty
with the Holy Spirit
and the Father be.

Dante Alighieri (1265-1321),
tr. R.A. Knox (1888-1957),
"Mary, Mother of Jesus"

Scripture

Again the Lord spoke to Ahaz, "Ask a sign of the Lord your God; let it be deep as Sheol or high as heaven." But Ahaz said, "I will not ask, and I will not put the Lord to the test." And he said, "Hear then, O house of David! Is it too little for you to weary men, that you weary my God also? Therefore the Lord himself will give you a sign. Behold, a young woman shall conceive and bear a son, and shall call his name Immanuel."

Isaiah 7:10-14

The Season of Christmas

⤥

These days, Christmas is not just a religious feast; it is also a seasonal mood, as people gradually get into the "Christmas spirit." Indeed, the religious aspect can be easily overlooked, with ever-increasing pleas for people to "put the Christ back into Christ-mas."

Perhaps surprisingly enough, Christmas was not an important time for the early Christians. The feast was the resurrection. But by the fourth century, a nativity festival was held in Rome on 25 December. The exact date of Jesus' birth is, of course, unknown, but it seems the Christians chose that date for a number of reasons. Among a range of theories put forward for this date is a connection between the winter solstice—when once again the days became longer and the dark nights shorter—and the celebration of this solstice by some pagans as the "birthday of the unconquered sun." Some experts would say that Christians in Rome "adopted" or even "adapted" these pagan ideas and began to celebrate their own feast of December 25th, the birthday of the light of the world. However the date was chosen, the feast was set to become a focal point for the church's year and was initially seen as, in fact, the start of the year.

And so in the midst of all the traditions that go to make up the sacred and secular mix in the "Christmas spirit"—cards, trees, presents, nativity plays, carols, holly, mistletoe, Santa Claus and the crib—our churches commemorate the birth of Christ at Midnight Mass and the Mass of Christmas Day.

Midnight Mass

"She laid him in a manger, because there was no room for them in the inn." I have sometimes wondered whether the inn-keeper ever discovered to whom he had refused entry into his inn. Poor man, it could not have been his fault, and he could not have known that the woman who knocked at his door was in fact carrying in her womb the Messiah, and, as we know, not just the Messiah, but God who had become man. No, he could not have known.

What about us, you and me? Do we refuse him entry into our lives? Do we slam the door in his face because we do not want him to question the way we live? Or is there simply no room for him? We have other preoccupations: our jobs, our leisure enjoyments, family responsibilities, and much else. And in any case we hear the voices of those many persons who tell us that religion is irrelevant, an unnecessary luxury for those that way inclined.

Now I believe that there is a space within each one of us which only God can fill. That was said by a former arch-bishop of Canterbury, Michael Ramsey. It is an important point, indeed a vital one, for a life without God is a stunted life. There is something missing. There is a void.

So we have to admit God into that space within us, which is for him. He must become part of our thinking, and an object of our desiring. He must dwell, so to speak, in our minds and hearts. Every time we celebrate Christmas we are reminded that God entered into our world in poverty and humility so as to dwell with us. We must welcome him. We must learn more about him, listen to his words as we read them in the gospels. All that Christ said and did as a man speaks to us of truths about God. They tell us what we mean to him and what he should mean to us. We must then get to know him as a person. This we do in the stillness of quiet reflection, which is prayer—brief moments stolen out of a busy day just to be alone with Christ.

Cardinal Hume, Midnight Mass, Westminster Cathedral, 1995

Prayer

Let us pray in the peace of Christmas midnight
that our joy in the birth of Christ will last for ever.
Father,
you make this holy night radiant
with the splendor of Jesus Christ our light.
We welcome him as Lord, the true light of the world.
Bring us to eternal joy in the kingdom of heaven,
where he lives and reigns with you and the Holy Spirit,
one God, for ever and ever.

Opening Prayer, Midnight Mass, Roman Missal

Lord Jesus Christ,
you came to a stable
when men looked in a palace;
you were born in poverty
when we might have anticipated riches;
King of all the earth,
you were content to visit one nation.
From beginning to end
you upturned our human values
and held us in suspense.
Come to us, Lord Jesus.
Do not let us take you for granted
or pretend that we ever fully understand you.
Continue to surprise us
so that, kept alert,
we are always ready
to receive you as Lord and to do your will.

Donald Hilton (b. 1932), "Lord of Surprises"

Scripture

In those days a decree went out from Caesar Augustus that all the world should be enrolled. This was the first enrollment, when Quirinius was governor of Syria. And all went to be enrolled, each to his own city. And Joseph also went up from Galilee, from the city of Nazareth, to Judea, to the city of David, which is called Bethlehem, because he was of the house and lineage of David, to be enrolled with Mary, his betrothed, who was with child. And while they were there, the time came for her to be delivered. And she gave birth to her first-born son, and wrapped him in swaddling cloths, and laid him in a manger, because there was no place for them in the inn.

And in that region there were shepherds out in the field, keeping watch over their flock by night. And an angel of the Lord appeared to them, and the glory of the Lord shone around them, and they were filled with fear. And the angel said to them, "Be not afraid; for behold, I bring you good news of a great joy which will come to all the people; for to you is born this day in the city of David a Savior, who is Christ the Lord. And this will be a sign for you: you will find a babe wrapped in swaddling cloths and lying in a manger." And suddenly there was with the angel a multitude of the heavenly host praising God and saying, "Glory to God in the highest, and on earth peace among men with whom he is pleased!"

Luke 2:1-14

Christmas Day

Today at this Mass we listened to St. John. We heard how he explained the coming of Christ: "And the Word was made flesh and dwelt amongst us," he wrote. He makes us think about the Word that was in the beginning, was with God, was indeed God. A word is one with the speaker but also separate when it is spoken. This is hard to understand, and in any case is an inadequate explanation of how the Son and the Father are related. For our purposes the simple truth suffices. The baby lying in the manger was God. St. John's mind soared where the human mind cannot go, like an eagle flying higher and higher beyond where the eye can see. But he, too, John, is unable to visualize what God is like; he is unable to describe to us the full meaning of the Second Person of the Blessed Trinity becoming a man.

So we listen to John and see his mind trying to understand the full reality of God becoming man. He cannot, and much less can we. We have to be humble. So, go and join the shepherds who went to see Jesus lying in a manger. Look at the child in the manger. Forget anything you have heard or read from people wanting to reduce Christmas to being no more than a myth, like a fairy tale, one to preserve because it is traditional and quaint. Kneel at the crib and profess your faith in the great truth that God became man and dwelt amongst us. You won't hear angels singing, "Glory to God in the highest, and peace

to persons of goodwill." No, you won't hear them, but
you will want to sing those same words when the great
truth of Christmas begins to dawn again in your mind.
That is what matters.

Cardinal Hume, Christmas Day Mass, Westminster Cathedral, 1997

Prayer

Father, all-powerful and ever-living God,
we do well always and everywhere to give you thanks
through Jesus Christ our Lord.
In the wonder of the incarnation
your eternal Word has brought to the eyes of faith
a new and radiant vision of your glory.
In him we see our God made visible
and so are caught up in love of the God we cannot see.

Preface of Christmas I, Roman Missal

**Our Loved ones
only go from us to God.**

And God is very near.

St. Augustine

DOMINICAN SHRINE OF ST. JUDE

1909 S. ASHLAND • CHICAGO, IL 60608
312-226-0020 • dominicans@preachers.org
www.shrineofsaintjude.com

And is it true? And is it true,
   This most tremendous tale of all,
Seen in a stained-glass window's hue,
   A Baby in an ox's stall?
The Maker of the stars and sea
Become a Child on earth for me?

And is it true? For if it is,
   No loving fingers tying strings
Around those tissued fripperies,
   The sweet and silly Christmas things,
Bath salts and inexpensive scent,
And hideous tie so kindly meant,

No love that in a family dwells,
   No carolling in frosty air,
Nor all the steeple-shaking bells
   Can with this single Truth compare—
That God was Man in Palestine
And lives to-day in Bread and Wine.

       John Betjeman (1906-84), "Christmas"

Scripture

In the beginning was the Word, and the Word was with God, and the Word was God. He was in the beginning with God; all things were made through him, and without him was not anything made that was made. In him was life, and the life was the light of men. The light shines in the darkness, and the darkness has not overcome it.

There was a man sent from God, whose name was John. He came for testimony, to bear witness to the light, that all might believe through him. He was not the light, but came to bear witness to the light.

The true light that enlightens every man was coming into the world. He was in the world, and the world was made through him, yet the world knew him not. He came to his own home, and his own people received him not. But to all who received him, who believed in his name, he gave power to become children of God; who were born, not of blood nor of the will of the flesh nor of the will of man, but of God.

And the Word became flesh and dwelt among us, full of grace and truth; we have beheld his glory, glory as of the only Son from the Father.

John 1:1-14

New Year's Day

The church's year begins with the First Sunday of Advent, not the first day of the calendar year. The church, then, begins its year by preparing for the coming of Jesus. But this does not mean to say that 1 January has no religious significance. The start of the year has the secular theme of seeing out the old and seeing in the new. The religious theme stems from the fact that 1 January still falls within the period of Christmas celebration (the octave, or week, of Christmas). On this day the Catholic Church celebrates both the feast of Mary, Mother of God, and a special day of prayer for peace throughout the world.

On New Year's Day every year I always say to myself: "Good, now we are beginning a new year it will be different and better than last year." And yet... and yet... it never turns out to be quite like that. We shall doubtless read and hear about scandals, about natural disasters and, alas, violence of every kind. And so, sadly, I reflect once again that we have proof enough that we are a fallen people. We are not as we should be. We can be cruel to each other, neglectful and uncaring. At least that is the impression given, until we realize that the world is also full of good people, many living lives of heroic goodness with integrity and who are caring and generous. We hear more of what is negative about our society rather than what is positive. Of course, we mustn't be naïve and pretend that there is no evil or sin in the world. There is. But don't forget all the good that is being done.

It is this thought that is uppermost in my mind today, New Year's Day: It is right to decry and lament the evil around us, but we must celebrate what is good. . . .

This leads me to another thought—to a possible New Year's resolution. It is this: To be prepared to change our-selves for the better. There is always a tendency within each one of us to be selfish, to be greedy, to be too materialistic in outlook and behavior. It is always a struggle to be good and to do good, but those unattractive tendencies have to be resisted every day. . . .

We must remember that every day there has to be a new start, in spite of yesterday's failures. And there is a more important point: We must recognize that achieving deep and lasting inner change is not just up to us. God is at work among and within us, prompting, inspiring us to become different, more pleasing to him. He wants us to become people who are kinder to each other, more respectful of each other, more generous to each other. If all of us made every effort to do this every day, the world would be a better place, and we would all be happier.

Cardinal Hume, BBC Prayer for the Day, New Year's Day, 1996

Prayer

As we begin this New Year
we ask you Father
to look on us with your love.
Help us to live lives pleasing to you
and help us to seek you in our prayers.
Help us, too, to be concerned for our neighbours,
to help them in their need.

Scripture

The Lord said to Moses, "Say to Aaron and his sons,
Thus you shall bless the people of Israel: You shall say to
them, The Lord bless you and keep you:
The Lord make his face to shine upon you,
and be gracious to you:
The Lord lift up his countenance upon you,
and give you peace."
So shall they put my name upon the people of Israel,
and I will bless them."

The book of Numbers recounts events under the leadership of Moses:
Numbers 6:22-27

Epiphany

Early in the new year, on 6 January, the church continues the Christmas season with the celebration of the feast of the Epiphany. It is the day whose popular links are with the story of the coming of the "three kings," the "magi," the "wise men." The popular story tells how they brought gifts to the baby Jesus: gold, frankincense, and myrrh.

Our English word "Epiphany" comes from the Greek *epiphanein*, meaning a "showing, appearance or revelation." The feast, then, shows that Jesus came as Savior not just for the Jews, but for all peoples, symbolized by the wise men. Although the gospel simply refers to "wise men from the East" (Matthew 2:1), the number three had cropped up in popular accounts by the third century, presumably because there were three gifts. By the sixth century the wise men had become kings, and ninth-century legends gave them names: Melchior, an old white man with a long white beard, bearing gold to Jesus; Caspar, a younger, darker man who gave Jesus frankincense; and Balthasar, a colored man, bearing myrrh.

Like the whole of the Christmas season, the Epiphany is a reminder that God has appeared among his people; the Word has truly become flesh.

Reflecting on today's feast, two considerations have struck me.
The first is the role of the star. It was there to guide
the three wise men to where they would find Christ, and
that thought reminds us of the importance of praying to

God to be given that inner star in our lives—the light of
faith—so that we may recognize, in the child born of the
Virgin Mary, God who became man, so that our assent to
that truth does not remain something merely on our lips
to which we vaguely give assent. It must be something
which fundamentally changes our lives. . . .

The second consideration is that we must go to Christ
and make our act of faith in him. But we must not go
empty-handed, we must go bearing our gifts.

Our gift of gold: the talents we have been given, the
gifts God has bestowed upon us, the opportunities that
have been given to us, realizing that we have to use these
in our own way for the Kingdom of God.

We must come to him, too, with our gift of frankincense,
that symbol of worship of God which has to be fundamental
in the life of each one of us; day by day to spend a short
time in acts of worship and obedience to God.

And our gift of myrrh: that is, the offering of our lives
entirely to God, prepared and ready to leave this world
when he so decrees; to live in this world building up the
Kingdom of God, but always remembering that our time
is limited and we must live in a state of preparedness.

So we celebrate this feast of the Epiphany, the
manifestation of Christ, true God and true man, and
we celebrate it worthily by the dedication of ourselves,
worshipping God and in the service of God, living in that
expectation of the joy that will be ours when we see him
face to face. . . .

Cardinal Hume, Feast of the Epiphany, 1993

Prayer

God has called you out of darkness,
into his wonderful light.
May you experience his kindness and blessings,
and be strong in faith, in hope, and in love.
Because you are followers of Christ,
who appeared on this day as a light shining in darkness,
may he make you a light to all your sisters and brothers.
The wise men followed the star,
and found Christ who is light from light.
May you too find the Lord
when your pilgrimage is ended.

Blessing on the Feast of the Epiphany, Roman Missal

Scripture

Now when Jesus was born in Bethlehem of Judea in the days of Herod the king, behold, wise men from the East came to Jerusalem, saying, "Where is he who has been born king of the Jews? For we have seen his star in the East, and have come to worship him." When Herod the king heard this, he was troubled, and all Jerusalem with him; and assembling all the chief priests and scribes of the people, he inquired of them where the Christ was to be born. They told him,"In Bethlehem of Judea; for so it is written by the prophet: 'And you, O Bethlehem, in the land of Judah, are by no means least among the rulers of Judah; for from you shall come a ruler who will govern my people Israel.'"

Then Herod summoned the wise men secretly and ascertained from them what time the star appeared; and he sent them to Bethlehem, saying, "Go and search diligently for the child, and when you have found him bring me word, that I too may come and worship him." When they had heard the king they went their way; and lo, the star which they had seen in the East went before them, till it came to rest over the place where the child was. When they saw the star, they rejoiced exceedingly with great joy; and going into the house they saw the child with Mary his mother, and they fell down and worshipped him. Then, opening their treasures, they offered him gifts, gold and frankincense and myrrh. And being warned in a dream not to return to Herod, they departed to their own country by another way.

Matthew 2:1-12

The Baptism of the Lord

One last feast closes the Christmas season. It is the Baptism of the Lord, celebrated on the Sunday after 6 January. Like the Epiphany, it is something of a revelation, as Jesus is baptized by John, and the voice of God the Father makes it clear that his Son is to bring healing and peace to all the nations.

At baptism the Father looks down on the baptized and sees in each one a family likeness, the likeness of Christ. Through baptism we become Christ-like—christened, so the Father now says of us: "This is my son, this is my daughter; in him, in her, I am well pleased." More profoundly still, St. Paul was to write: "It is no longer I who live, but Christ who lives in me" (Galatians 2:20). We go in search of ways to describe the great dignity which baptism confers on us, and to some extent we flounder, unable to find the right thoughts or adequate words to describe the beauty of a person who has been baptized. Perhaps we hesitate to identify ourselves with St. Peter's words: "You are a chosen race, a royal priesthood, a holy nation, God's own people" (1 Peter 2:9).

Cardinal Hume, Easter Vigil, 1991

There is in us a thirst for God, beautifully expressed in the psalm: "Like the deer that thirsts for running streams, so my soul is yearning, is yearning for you, my God. My soul is thirsting for God, the God of my life. . . ." (Psalm 42:1-2).

But let me tell you of another thirst: It is God's thirst for us. God wants us to be cleansed from sin. God wants to give us life, and does so by giving us the great sacrament of baptism.

It is a beautiful thought to remember that God begins the quenching of his thirst for us by giving the water of baptism to make us thirst more for him.

Cardinal Hume, Easter Vigil, 1995

Prayer

Let us pray that we will be faithful to our baptism.
Almighty, eternal God,
when the Spirit descended upon Jesus
at his baptism in the Jordan,
you revealed him as your own beloved Son.
Keep us, your children born of water and the Spirit,
faithful to our calling.

Opening Prayer, Feast of the Baptism of the Lord, Roman Missal

Scripture

In those days Jesus came from Nazareth of Galilee and was baptized by John in the Jordan. And when he came up out of the water, immediately he saw the heavens opened and the Spirit descending upon him like a dove; and a voice came from heaven, "Thou art my beloved Son; with thee I am well pleased."

Mark 1:9-11

Therefore, if any one is in Christ, he is a new creation; the old has passed away; behold, the new has come.

St. Paul's second letter to the people of Corinth, written maybe c. AD 58: 2 Corinthians 5:17

The Journey Continues

❧

Cardinal George Basil Hume was invited by the United States Bishops' Conference to address their special assembly in June 1999. Although he completed the text of his speech before his final illness was diagnosed, he was unable to travel to the United States to deliver it in person. However, he recorded the speech on video and it was broadcast to the assembly of bishops on June 18, 1999, the day after Cardinal Hume died. This quotation is taken from the end of that speech.

As the church makes its pilgrim way through history, it must constantly be purified and renewed. . . . I would like to suggest that we look again at a remarkable passage in *Evangelii Nuntiandi*, written by Pope Paul VI in 1975: "The world is calling for evangelizers to speak to it of a God whom the evangelists themselves should know and be familiar with as if they could see the invisible" (*Evangelii Nuntiandi*, 76). Note those last words, "as if they could see the invisible." That paradox says something very important. With the eyes of faith you have to look beyond the visible things that we can see to contemplate the invisible ones that we cannot (Romans 1:19).

Ten years later Pope John Paul II... said that we need heralds of the gospel who "are experts in humanity, who know the depths of the human heart, who can share the joys and hopes, the agonies and distress of people today, but are at the same time contemplatives who have fallen in love with God."

All of us... must become more deeply spiritual. Prayer is a priority for all of us. Today people are crying out to be taught how to pray and to be given a deeper meaning of what life is about. People are looking for spirituality. A few years ago I had to give an important talk to a large number of top professionals, company directors, and the like. The topic they requested was "Spirituality and Morality." That is the need today. People want to hear about God and to hear about their relationship with him.

We want our people to walk as if they could see the invisible and to have fallen in love with God. The pilgrim people of God, journeying into the next millennium, must meet again that pilgrim coming in the opposite direction, him who is the way, the truth and the life, whom to see is to have seen the Father. Christ must be born afresh into our world.

Cardinal Hume

References

Richard Garrard, *Love on the Cross*, Kevin Mayhew, Bury St. Edmunds, 1995, pp. 21 (adapted), 57, 63, 78.

Cardinal Basil Hume, *Light in the Lord—Reflections on Priesthood*, St. Paul Publications, Slough, 1991, p. 162.

Cardinal Basil Hume, *The Mystery of Love*, Hodder & Stoughton, London, 1996, pp. 18, 31-32.

Cardinal Basil Hume, *The Mystery of the Cross*, Darton, Longman & Todd, London, 1998, p. 20, 72-73.

Cardinal Basil Hume, *The Mystery of the Incarnation*, Darton, Longman & Todd, London, 1999, p. 151.

Cardinal Basil Hume, *To Be a Pilgrim—A Spiritual Notebook*, St. Paul Publications, Slough, 1984.